Brilliant Model Ans

C000293687

Published by

Educationzone Ltd

London N21 3YA
United Kingdom

British Library Cataloguing in Publication Data:

A catalogue record for this publication is available from the British Library.

978-1-906468-65-1

Email us for further information:

info@psychologyzone.co.uk

You can email Nick Savva directly at:

nicksavva@live.co.uk

For more information:
Visit our website for exam questions and answers, teaching resources, books and much more:

www.psychologyzone.co.uk

Content for model answers

Please note: this book is not endorsed by or affiliated to the AQA exam board.

Important information

 *Do not skip this page!*

■ The 'unpredictable' exam is more 'predictable' than you think

This guide is part of Psychologyzone's Brilliant Model Answers series covering A-level Psychology. Use it alongside the Psychologyzone series Brilliant Exam Notes to get the best out of your learning.

This guide covering the topic of Social Influences provides a full set of exam-style questions and model answers to help you do well in the exam. After all, your psychology exam is based on answering questions – what better than to have a book that already has the answers for you!

The exam board has deliberately developed the A-level Psychology specification so that the questions are to some extent 'unpredictable' in order to discourage students from attempting to rote-learn (memorise answers) using pre-prepared questions. This makes it difficult to predict what's going to be asked.

We have tried to make the unpredictable 'predictable'...

There are over 100 model answers in this book. We have covered most of the different types of question they can ask you for each topic on the specification. You can adapt the model answers provided to most types of questions set in the exam.

■ Some of your model answers seem very long. Why?

Some of the answers are much longer responses than you are expected to write in the exam to get top marks. This is deliberate. We have written them in this way to enable you to have a better understanding of the theories, concepts, studies and so on. If you do not write as much, don't panic; you don't need all of the content to achieve a good grade.

As you may be using this as a study book, we thought we'd write the model answers in a way that you can also revise from them, so we sometimes expand on explanations or give an example to help you understand a topic better.

Many of the model answers start by repeating the question; in the real exam you do not need to waste time doing this – just get stuck in!

Remember - in your exam, your answers will be marked according to how well you demonstrate the set assessment objectives (AOs); therefore, we have tried to provide model responses that show you how to demonstrate the required know-how for these AOs. Each example provides you with 'indicative content': in other words, the response gives you an idea of points you could make to achieve maximum marks; it doesn't mean these are points you must make. The purpose of these model answers is to inspire you and demonstrate the standard required to achieve top marks.

Exam skills

How will your answer be assessed?

Your teachers will have explained that your answers in the examination will be assessed on what examiners call assessment objectives (AO). If you can familiarise yourself with these AO, this will help you write more effective answers and achieve a higher grade in your exam. There are three assessment objectives called AO1, AO2 and AO3.

By now, your teachers should have given you a lot of practice exam questions and techniques on how to answer them. The aim of this book is not to teach you these skills, but to show you how this is done – to model the answers for you.

Just to remind you, below are the AQA assessment objectives:

 AO1 **Knowledge and understanding**

Demonstrate knowledge and understanding of scientific ideas, processes, techniques and procedures

What does this mean?

The ability to describe psychological theories, concepts, research studies (e.g. aim, procedures, findings and conclusions) and key terms. The exam questions can cover anything that is named on the specification.

Example

Explain the process of synaptic transmission.   **[5 marks]**

Outline the role of the somatosensory centre in the brain.   **[3 marks]**

 AO2 **Application**

Apply knowledge and understanding of scientific ideas, processes, techniques and procedures:

- in a theoretical context
- in a practical context
- when handling qualitative data
- when handling quantitative data.

What does this mean?

Application questions require you to apply what you have learnt about in Psychology (theories, concepts and studies) to a scenario (situation) often referred to as 'stem' material. A scenario will be a text extract or quote given in the question. You are treated as a psychologist and you need to explain what is going on in the situation from what you have learnt.

Example

Chris suffered a stroke to the left hemisphere of his brain, damaging Broca's area and the motor cortex.

Using your knowledge of the functions of Broca's area and the motor cortex, describe the problems that Chris is likely to experience. **[4 marks]**

 Evaluation

Analyse, interpret and evaluate scientific information, ideas and evidence, including in relation to issues, to:

- make judgements and reach conclusions
- develop and refine practical design and procedures.

What does this mean?

Evaluation simply means assessing the 'value' (hence 'evaluation' of a theory or study you have been describing. There are many ways you can evaluate theories or studies. For students, evaluation often takes the form of the strengths and weaknesses of the theory and/or study, but evaluation can also be in a form of 'commentary' (neither strength nor weakness but more in the form of an 'analysis' – which is still an evaluation).

Example

Outline one strength and one limitation of post-mortem examination. **[2 marks + 2 marks]**

The different types of exam questions

We have grouped the exam questions into four different types:

Identification questions	Multiple-choice questions, match key words with a definition, tick boxes or place information in some order or in a box.
Short-response questions	Questions worth up to 6 marks (e.g. 1, 2, 3, 4, 5 or 6 marks). These are often questions asking you to 'outline', 'explain', or 'evaluate' a theory or a study.
Application questions	These require you to apply the psychological knowledge you have learnt (theories, concepts and studies) to a real-life scenario given in the exam question.
Long-response question	These deal with long answers worth over 6 marks (8, 12 or 16 marks). The long-response answers found in this book will be mainly for 16-mark questions.

How the model answers are structured

We have tried to structure your learning by breaking down the model answers into four distinct categories

Key terms, concepts, and theories that are named on the AQA specification are covered by the identification and short-response questions (e.g. explain what is meant by the term...).

Research questions asking you to outline a study, describe a theory or give an evaluation are covered by short-response questions (e.g. briefly outline one study that has...).

Application questions require you to apply your knowledge to a made-up scenario (situation) and are covered under application questions.

Essay questions 'Outline and evaluate', or 'Discuss'-type questions are covered under long-response questions. Some long-response questions also require the application of knowledge.

Specification: Biopsychology

Biopsychology specification

- The divisions of the nervous system: central and peripheral (somatic and autonomic).

- The structure and function of sensory, relay and motor neurons. The process of synaptic transmission, including reference to neurotransmitters, excitation and inhibition.

- The function of the endocrine system: glands and hormones.

- The fight-or-flight response including the role of adrenaline.

- Localisation of function in the brain and hemispheric lateralisation: motor, somatosensory, visual, auditory and language centres; Broca's and Wernicke's areas, split brain research. Plasticity and functional recovery of the brain after trauma.

- Ways of studying the brain: scanning techniques, including functional magnetic resonance

- Imaging (fMRI); electroencephalogram (EEGs) and event-related potentials (ERPs); post-mortem examinations.

- Biological rhythms: circadian, infradian and ultradian and the difference between these rhythms.

- The effect of endogenous pacemakers and exogenous zeitgebers on the sleep/wake cycle.

Nervous system

Identification questions

Q1 Complete the following sentence.

Circle one letter only. **[1 mark]**

Motor neurons carry information

    A. away from the brain.

    B. both to and from the brain.

    C. towards the brain.

    D. within the brain.

Q2 Which one of the following body responses is the results from the action of the sympathetic division of the autonomic nervous system?

Circle one letter only. **[1 mark]**

    A. Decreased pupil size

    B. Increased digestion

    C. Increased heart rate

    D. Increased salivation

Q3 Complete the following sentence.

Circle one letter only. **[1 mark]**

The somatic nervous system:

    A. comprises of two sub-systems.

    B. connects the central nervous system and the senses.

    C. consists of the brain and spinal cord.

    D. controls involuntary responses.

Q4 Read the following statements and decide whether they are TRUE or FALSE:

Circle one letter for each question **[2 marks]**

    (a) Motor neurons carry messages to the central nervous system.

       A. TRUE

       B. FALSE

    b) The nucleus of a neuron is found outside the cell body (soma).

       A. TRUE

       B. FALSE

Q5 Which two of the following statements about the divisions of the nervous system are correct?

Circle two letters only. **[2 marks]**

    A. The fight-or-flight response occurs when the parasympathetic division controls functioning.

    B. The central nervous system consists of the brain and spinal cord.

    C. Sensory, relay and motor neurons are all controlled by the somatic nervous system.

    D. Sensory neurons carry messages from the central nervous system.

    E. The somatic nervous system controls voluntary movement.

Q6 Label the two areas of the synapse in the diagram below.

Write the appropriate letters in the answers in the boxes provided. **[2 marks]**

In the human nervous system...

    A.   Axon

    B.   Dendrites

    C.   Neurotransmitters

    D.   Receptor sites

    E.   Vesicle

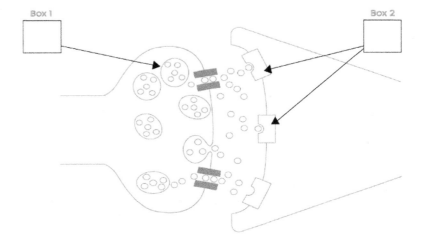

Name the types of neurons labelled A, B and C on the figure below.
Write your answers in the boxes provided   **[3 marks]**

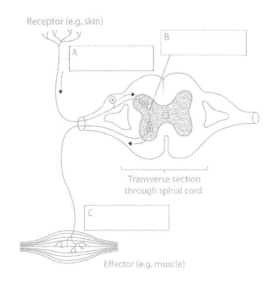

The diagram shows three different types of neuron.   **[3 marks]**

Use the letters A, B, and C, to answer the following questions.

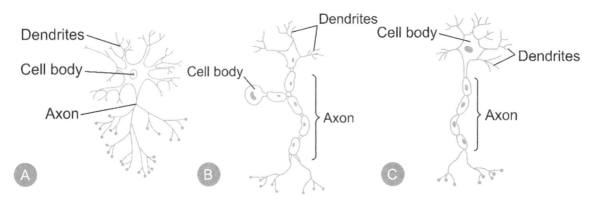

a. Which neuron is only found in the brain/visual system/spinal cord?

Circle one letter.

A   B   C

b. Which neuron carries nerve impulses from the brain/spinal cord to muscles/glands?

Circle one letter.

A   B   C

c. Which neuron carries nerve impulses between neurons?

Circle one letter.

A   B   C

Short-response questions

Q9 Identify two components of the central nervous system. **[2 marks]**

The brain and spinal cord.

Q10 Outline the role of the central nervous system. **[4 marks]**

The central nervous system (CNS) comprises the brain and spinal cord and has two main functions: to control our behaviour and to regulate the body's physiological processes. To do this, the brain receives information from the sensory receptors (e.g. eyes and skin) from the environment and then sends messages to the body's muscles (e.g. arms, legs) and glands. These messages are sent through the spinal cord, a collection of nerve cells that are attached to the brain and run the length of the spinal column.

Q11 Identify two divisions of the autonomic nervous system. **[2 marks]**

The sympathetic nervous system and the parasympathetic nervous system.

Q12 Outline the role of the somatic nervous system. **[4 marks]**

The somatic nervous system (SNS) is responsible for transmitting sensory information via the central nervous system (CNS) to other areas of the body. The SNS does this by carrying sensory information from the environment (e.g. eyes, sound, skin), via the nerves and sensory neurons to the CNS (spinal cord and brain), which then sends the information to other areas of the body (e.g. skeletal muscles), using motor neurons. The SNS is also involved in reflex actions without the involvement of the central nervous system, which allows the reflex to occur very quickly.

Q13 Outline the role of the autonomic nervous system. **[4 marks]**

The role of the autonomic nervous system (ANS) is to regulate involuntary actions of the internal body organs, such as heartbeat, glands, digestion, breathing, without us being consciously aware of this happening. The ANS has two parts: the sympathetic and parasympathetic systems. These systems work on the same organs but have opposite effects. The sympathetic system is primarily involved in responses that help us deal with threats or emergencies by increasing heart rate, breathing and blood pressure, etc. The parasympathetic system is involved with energy conservation and slows down physiological activity (heart rate, blood pressure, breathing, etc.).

Q14 Identify the two components of the peripheral nervous system and explain two differences in their organisation and/or functions. **[4 marks]**

Two components of the peripheral nervous system are the somatic nervous system (SNS) and the autonomic nervous system (ANS).

One difference is that the SNS has sensory and motor pathways, while the ANS is purely a motor pathway. Another difference is that the SNS controls skeletal muscle, movement, whereas the ANS controls internal organs and glands of the body.

Q15 Briefly give two differences between the autonomic nervous system and the somatic nervous system. **[4 marks]**

One difference is that the autonomic nervous system is involuntary, not under our conscious control, whereas the somatic nervous system is under our conscious control.

Another difference is that the autonomic nervous system controls our smooth muscles (e.g. intestines and stomach) and normal glands, whereas the somatic nervous system controls the muscles attached to our skeleton.

Q16 Information can only travel in one direction at a synapse.

Explain why neurons can only transmit information in one direction at a synapse.

WATCH OUT: This question is asking you why neurons can travel one way – you need to explain it. Do not start describing the process of synaptic transmission as this is not what the question is asking. **[3 marks]**

The reason why information can only travel in one direction in the synapse is due to the specific function of different parts of the neuron. For example, at the end of the pre-synaptic neuron are synaptic vesicles that contain neurotransmitters, these synaptic vesicles can only release the neurotransmitters at the pre-synaptic membrane into the synaptic gap. Also, the receptors to receive the neurotransmitters in the synapse are only present on the post-synaptic membrane which enables the information to be transmitted onto the next neuron. This would make it impossible for information to flow in any other direction.

Q17 Explain the process of synaptic transmission. **[5 marks]**

Synaptic transmission is the process of sending information from one neuron to the next to activate a brain function or body parts (e.g. muscle or gland). Initially, the information travels down the axon of the neuron as an electrical message (known as an action potential) towards the axon terminal that contains synaptic vesicles. These vesicles contain chemical messengers known as neurotransmitters (molecules), whose job it is to transmit messages. The action potential causes the vesicle to move towards the pre-synaptic terminals and release the neurotransmitters that carry the information across the synaptic cleft. The neurotransmitters reach the dendrite of the next neuron and attach themselves to the receptor sites on the post-synaptic cell, where the chemical is converted back into an electrical impulse. Neurotransmitters can produce excitatory or inhibitory effects on the post-synaptic neuron cell (receiving neuron).

If there are more excitatory neurotransmitters (than inhibitory), this means that the receiving post-synaptic neuron is more likely to fire and generate an electrical impulse, which will then go on to influence our behaviour. If there are more inhibitory neurotransmitters (than excitatory) sent to the post-synaptic neuron, it is less likely to fire and generate electrical impulses, and transmission of electrical impulses comes to a halt, again affecting our behaviour (e.g. inducing sleep or calming down).

Q18 Briefly outline how excitation and inhibition are involved in synaptic transmission.

WATCH OUT: Remember the actual excitation and inhibition (firing) of the neuron occur at the post-synaptic cell, not before it (e.g. synapse cleft (gap)). **[4 marks]**

Neurotransmitters can produce excitatory or inhibitory effects on the post-synaptic neuron cell. If there are more excitatory than inhibitory neurotransmitters, the net effect on the post-synaptic neuron is excitatory, which means the receiving post-synaptic neuron is more likely to fire and generate an electrical impulse, which will then go on to influence our behaviour. If there are more inhibitory than excitatory neurotransmitters, the net effect on the post-synaptic neuron is inhibitory, which means that the neuron is less likely to fire an electrical impulse, and transmission of electrical impulses is halted, again affecting our behaviour (e.g. inducing sleep or calming down).

Application question

Q19 Jack is drilling a hole in a wall. He feels the drill hit a large metal pipe, which made the drill jolt, so he stops drilling immediately.

Explain how sensory, relay and motor neurons would function in this situation. **[4 marks]**

The sensory receptors in Jack's hand would sense the jolt of the drill hitting the metal pipe. A signal will be sent through the nerve fibres of the sensory neurons to the spinal cord and then to the brain.

The sensory neuron then connects with the relay neuron, which is mostly found in the spinal cord and the brain. Relay neurons allow sensory and motor neurons to communicate. Here the relayed neuron would be involved in the analysis of the sensation, which means it will decide how to respond to it.

If the motor neurons are stimulated by the relay neurons, the motor neuron fibres will send electrical impulses (messages) from the brain to the effector (muscles), which produces a response. Here, the message from the brain instructs Jack's arm muscles to stop drilling.

Endocrine system

Identification question

Q20 The master gland of the endocrine system is the:

Circle one letter only. **[1 mark]**

    A. hypothalamus.

    B. pituitary gland.

    C. thyroid gland.

    D. adrenal gland.

Short-response questions

Q21 Briefly explain two functions of the endocrine system. **[4 marks]**

One function of the endocrine system is to control and regulate bodily functions. For example, the adrenal gland regulates the amount of cortisol that controls the body's stress response.

Another function of the endocrine system is to act as a communication system. The endocrine system does this by releasing chemical messengers into the bloodstream to regulate certain cells and organs of the body. For example, when the thyroid gland produces thyroxine hormone, this affects how fast your heart beats.

Q22 Identify two glands that form part of the endocrinal system and outline their functions. **[4 marks]**

One gland is the thyroid gland. The function of this gland is to release a hormone called thyroxine, which is responsible for regulating the body's metabolic rate and heart rate.

Another gland is the adrenal gland. The function of this gland is to release adrenaline and noradrenaline, which cause physiological changes associated with the fight-or-flight response.

The endocrine system is a network of glands throughout the body that manufacture and secrete hormones, which are chemical messengers, into the bloodstream. Each gland in the endocrine system produces different hormones, which regulate the activity of specific organs and tissues in the body. The pituitary gland, known as the 'master gland', of the endocrine system, secretes a stimulating hormone into the bloodstream that targets the other glands and determines the levels of hormones released by each gland. The endocrine system is regulated by a feedback-loop system to keep the body's physiological responses constant. For example, as levels of hormones rise in the bloodstream, the pituitary gland sends the 'secreting' hormone to the targeted glands to reduce the secretion of hormones and prevents hormone levels from becoming too high. As a result, a stable concentration of hormones circulates in the body.

Fight-or-flight response

Identification questions

Q24 Which two of the following statements about the fight-or-flight response are correct?

Circle two letters only.

During the fight-or-flight response: **[2 marks]**

    A. there is a decrease in the release of adrenaline.

    B. the flow of blood is diverted from the surface of the skin.

    C. the process of digestion is inhibited.

    D. the parasympathetic division is in control of function.

    E. there is a reduction in the rate of respiration.

Short-response questions

Q25 Below are features of the body's fight-or-flight response to an immediate dangerous situation.

Select three from the list that are linked to an immediate fight-or-flight response. **[3 marks]**

    A. Adrenal medulla

    B. Noradrenaline

    C. Adrenaline

    D. Cortisol/corticosteroids

    E. Adrenocorticotrophic hormone (ACTH)

Q26 Explain what is meant by the fight-or-flight response. **[3 marks]**

The fight-or-flight response enables us to react quickly to life-threatening situations. When we are confronted with a threatening situation, the amygdala is activated, which sends a distress signal to the hypothalamus. The hypothalamus then sends a signal to the adrenal medulla gland to release the hormone adrenaline into the bloodstream, which activates the sympathetic nervous system (SNS). The SNS triggers physiological changes, e.g. in heart rate and breathing, which help the person to prepare a fight-or-flight response (stay and fight or run away).

Q27 Explain what is meant by the fight-or-flight response.

WATCH OUT: When explaining the fight -or -flight response, write about the process of how the body becomes prepared for it and how the body responds (e.g. increaseincreased heart rate) to these changes. **[6 marks]**

The fight-or-flight response enables us to react quickly to life-threatening situations. When we are confronted with a threatening situation, the amygdala is activated, which sends a distress signal to the hypothalamus. The hypothalamus prepares the body for response by sending signals through the autonomic nervous system (ANS) to the adrenal medulla gland to release the hormone adrenaline into your bloodstream. The adrenaline then activates the sympathetic nervous system (SNS), which prepares us for the fight-or-flight response by bringing physiological changes in our body. The physiological effects of adrenaline on the body are an increase in heart rate and constricting blood vessels (e.g. arteries, veins), thereby increasing the rate of blood flow and raising blood pressure (providing oxygen and energy to the brain, organs and skeletal muscles more quickly); increase in muscle tension; increase in breathing rate (increase in oxygen); reduction of blood supply to non-essential functions (e.g. skin, digestive system, kidneys); increase in respiration (to regulate body temperature); and dilation of the pupils (to allow more light to enter the eyes, especially at night). Adrenaline also triggers the release of glucose from the liver into your bloodstream, supplying energy to the body. Once the threat is over, the parasympathetic nervous system (PNS) takes control and attempts to reduce your 'flight or fight' response by slowing down your heart rate, reducing your blood pressure, decreasing the release of glucose, allowing digestion to restart, and bringing your body back to a 'normal' resting state.

Q28 Outline the role of adrenaline in the fight-or-flight response. **[4 marks]**

The role of the hormone adrenaline is to speed up the body's physiological response to a threatening situation. Adrenaline causes an increase in heart rate and constricts blood vessels (e.g. arteries, veins), thereby increasing the rate of blood flow and raising blood pressure (providing oxygen and energy more quickly) and increasing the breathing rate (increase in oxygen). Adrenaline also triggers the release of glucose (sugar) from the liver into your bloodstream, supplying energy to the body to help the fight-or-flight response.

Q29 Adrian hates flying on aeroplanes. As soon as it is time for the plane to take off, his heart starts beating really fast, and he begins to sweat. After take-off, once the plane is airborne, Adrian feels better, and his heart stops beating as fast, and the sweating stops.

Using your knowledge of the body's response to stress, explain why Adrian experienced these changes and:

   a. the body's reaction during take-off;

   b. the body's reaction after take-off. **[2 marks + 2 marks]**

   a. The plane taking off would be an acute stressor for Adrian, causing the sympathetic branch of the autonomic nervous system to activate and trigger the body into the 'fight-or-flight' response, which in turn causes the heart to beat faster and the body to sweat.

   b. After the plane takes off, the acute stress for Adrian is over. The parasympathetic nervous system takes control and attempts to reduce the 'flight or fight' response by slowing down the heart rate and bringing the body back to a normal relaxed state.

Q30 You are a passenger in a car when the driver suddenly slams on the brakes to avoid hitting a dog. Your breathing quickens, your mouth is dry, and you have a feeling of 'butterflies' in your stomach. But after a few minutes, these physical changes start to disappear.

Using your knowledge of the body's response to stress, explain why you are likely to have experienced:

   a. the changes that occurred in the first 30 seconds;

   b. the changes that occurred after a few minutes. **[2 marks + 2 marks]**

   a. The sympathetic branch of the autonomic nervous system was triggered as a response to the imminent danger of hitting the dog. This brought about physiological changes to the body, such as faster breathing and rapid heart rate (providing oxygen more quickly for the body) and dry mouth and butterflies (shutting the digestive system down), preparing the body for a 'fight-or-flight' response.

   b. After the potential threat had passed, the parasympathetic nervous system would reduce the 'fight-or-flight' response and restore the normal physiological functioning of the body back to a normal relaxed state.

Q31 The fight-or-flight response enabled our ancestors to survive but can be less helpful in response to more modern stressors.

Explain how the body responds during fight or flight and why this could be unhelpful in a driving test situation. **[4 marks]**

The fight-or-flight response causes adrenaline to be released into the bloodstream, which can cause increased production of sweat and an increase in heart rate and breathing, as well as muscles tensing up, which could be off-putting and unhelpful during a driving test. For example, having sweaty hands may make it harder to grip the steering wheel, or having tensed muscles may force you to make an erratic movement, which could lead to an error with changing gears or using the pedals. Furthermore, the fight-or-flight response allows a quick reaction to either 'fight' the threat or run away (flight) from a dangerous/stressful situation. Neither of these options would be helpful in a driving test because if you ran away (flight) or attacked (fight) the instructor, you would fail your driving test.

Q32 You are just about to cross the road when a car comes speeding round the corner and narrowly misses you. Afterwards, standing safely on the pavement, you notice that your mouth is very dry, your breathing is very fast, and your heart is thumping.

Using your knowledge of the body's response to stress, explain why you are likely to have experienced these changes. **[4 marks]**

The adrenaline hormone was released into the blood as a result of a perceived threat of a speeding car. The effects of the adrenaline triggered an increase in heart rate (providing oxygen and energy to the brain, organs and skeletal muscles more quickly), an increase in breathing rate (increase in oxygen supply), and a very dry mouth (saliva production is reduced linked to the digestive system 'shutting down'). These body changes help prepare the body for 'fight' or 'flight' from the speeding car.

Q33 You are walking home at night. It is dark, and you hear someone running behind you. Your breathing quickens, your mouth dries, and your heart pounds. Then you hear your friend call out, "Hey, wait for me! We can walk back together." Your breathing slows down, and after a couple of minutes, you are walking home calmly with your friend.

Explain the actions of the autonomic nervous system. Refer to the description above in your answer. **[4 marks]**

The sympathetic branch of the autonomic nervous system was triggered as a response to the perceived threat of imminent danger (person in the dark). This brings about physiological changes in the body in response to the threat, such as faster breathing, rapid heart rate and dry mouth, ready for a 'fight-or- flight' response. After the potential threat has passed, the parasympathetic nervous system will reduce the 'fight-or-flight' response and restore the normal physiological functioning of the body back to a normal relaxed state (your breathing slows, and you are walking home calmly).

Long-response question

Outline and evaluate the fight-or-flight response. **[16 marks]**

The fight-or-flight response enables us to react quickly to life-threatening situations. The fight-or-flight response evolved from our evolutionary past, where humans were constantly faced with stressors in the form of physical danger (e.g. predators, natural disasters) and a quick behavioural response was required, either by fighting off the threat (fight) or running away (flight) to survive. The fight-or-flight response evolved because it increased our chances of surviving and reproducing and is therefore adaptive. When exposed to a threatening situation, the sensory information is immediately sent to the amygdala, which sends a distress signal to the hypothalamus. The hypothalamus prepares the body for response by sending signals through the autonomic nervous system (ANS) to the adrenal medulla gland to release the hormone adrenaline into the bloodstream. The adrenaline then activates the sympathetic nervous system (SNS), which prepares us for the 'fight-or-flight' response by bringing physiological changes in our body. Some of the physiological effects of adrenaline on the body are an increase in heart rate, constricted blood vessels, which increase the rate of blood flow and raise blood pressure (providing oxygen and energy to the body more quickly), and an increase in breathing rate. Adrenaline also triggers the release of glucose (sugar) from the liver into the bloodstream, supplying energy to the body. Once the threat is over, the parasympathetic nervous system (PNS) takes control and attempts to reduce the 'fight-or-flight' response by slowing down heart rate and blood pressure, decreasing the release of glucose, allowing digestion to restart, and bringing your body back to a 'normal' resting state.

Research into the body's response has had positive implications in terms of our understanding of stress and illness. In ancestral times, the fight-or-flight response evolved as a survival mechanism to real life-threatening physical stressors (e.g. predators). In the modern world, although life-threatening physical situations still occur (although not in the form of predators), the fight-or-flight response is now more often triggered by daily social stresses (relationships, finances, public speaking, etc.), rather than by physical danger. Research has shown that this constant intense biological reaction to psychological stress can lead to physical health damage. For example, repeated activation of the stress response can promote the formation of artery-clogging deposits in the heart, which leads to the hardening and narrowing of the arteries, resulting in a higher risk of a heart attack. This shows there is a mismatch between the body's reaction and psychological stress and suggests that the fight-or-flight response is a maladaptive response in modern-day life, as it can have negative consequences on our health.

However, one criticism of our understanding of the fight-or-flight response is that individual differences can modify how the body responds to stress, for example, personality, culture and gender, and it is not solely a physiological response. For instance, research suggests that the fight-or-flight response is typically a male response to a threat and that females adopt a 'tend and befriend' response in threatening or stressful situations. Taylor et al. (2000) suggested that women have evolved to have a completely different system for coping with stress because they are the primary caregivers for children. They are more likely to protect their offspring (tend) and form alliances with other women (befriend), than fight or flee. Furthermore, fleeing too readily at any sign of danger would put a female's child at risk. This shows that individual differences can modify the effects of stress, which means there is no common physiological body response to a threat.

The above criticism also shows the fight-or-flight explanation as reductionist (oversimplified). This is because applying physiological mechanisms to explain human behaviour means we are reducing behaviour and our thinking processes to a biological (hormonal) level. Despite the importance of biological processes in determining our behaviour, this seems too simple an explanation for the reaction of people to stress, as other factors may equally influence how we respond to pressures. For example, cognitive factors, such as how we perceive various threatening situations, will determine how intense and how long our response will be. This suggests that our thought processes play a big role in our fight-or-flight response, and the explanation may not adequately account for how people manage stress in their lives.

Further criticism of the fight-or-flight hypothesis as an explanation is that it is too simplistic. Gray (1988) suggested that most animals, including humans, display the 'freeze response' before a fight-or-flight when faced with a threat. This is essentially a phase in which the animals are hyper-vigilant, which allows them to assess the situation before they decide to fight or flee. 'Freezing' is an adaptive response because it focuses attention and makes us look for new information to choose the best response to a particular threat. This suggests that the fight-or-flight response is not the only way animals and humans respond to a threat.

Localisation of brain function

Identification questions

Q35 Below are four functional areas of the brain. Choose one area of the brain that matches each function and write A, B, C or D in the box next to it.

Use each letter only once. **[3 marks]**

    A. Broca's area

    B. Wernicke's area

    C. Motor area

    D. Somatosensory area

       i.   Area of the brain responsible for production of speech ☐

      ii.   Area of the brain responsible for comprehension of speech ☐

     iii. Area of the brain responsible for inputs from touch ☐

Q36 Psychologists have identified many areas of cortical specialisation in the brain.

Below is a diagram of the human brain. Identify three areas of cortical specialisation by writing A, B, C or D in each of the boxes that are provided. Use a different letter for each box.

[3 marks]

This includes:

    A. The motor cortex

    B. The auditory cortex

    C. The visual cortex

    D. The somatosensory cortex

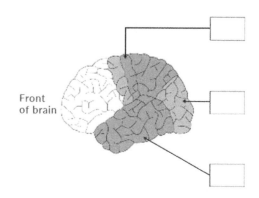

Q37 The image below shows the left hemisphere of the human brain. Six areas of cortical specialisation are labelled A, B, C, D, E and F. **[5 marks]**

Using your knowledge of localisation of function in the brain, identify the area of cortical specialisation. Write the letter in each of the boxes that are provided. Use a different letter for each box.

(a) Broca's area ☐

(b) Somatosensory cortex ☐

(c) Visual cortex ☐

(d) Wernicke's area ☐

(e) Motor cortex ☐

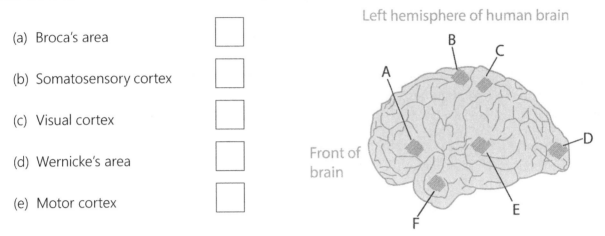

Left hemisphere of human brain

Front of brain

Short-response questions

Q38 Explain what is meant by localisation of brain function and give one example. **[2 marks]**

Localisation of the function of the brain refers to the view that the brain has specific areas or regions that are responsible for certain psychological and physiological functions. For example, the Broca area is found on the left side of the frontal lobe and is considered to play a vital role in speech production.

Q39 Outline the nature of the motor centre in the brain. **[3 marks]**

The motor centre is responsible for controlling and carrying out voluntary movements. The motor centre is located in the frontal lobe that runs across both cerebral hemispheres, with the centre on one side of the brain controlling the muscles on the opposite side of the body. Different parts of the motor centre control different parts of the body.

Q40 Outline the role of the somatosensory centre in the brain. **[3 marks]**

The somatosensory centre can be found in the parietal lobe of the brain. Its role is to detect and process sensory information (sensations) arising from receptors positioned throughout the body that are responsible for detecting sensations such touch, pressure, pain, and temperature.

When sensory receptors detect one of these sensations, the information is sent to the thalamus and then to the primary somatosensory cortex area in the brain.

Q41 Outline the role of the visual centre in the brain. **[3 marks]**

The visual centre (visual cortex) is found in the occipital lobe of the brain and its role is to process different types of visual information (e.g. colour, shape, and movement). The brain has two visual centres, one in each cerebral hemisphere. The visual centre in the right cerebral hemisphere receives its information from the left visual field (left eye), while the visual centre in the left cerebral hemisphere receives its input from the right visual field (right eye).

Q42 Outline the role of the auditory centre in the brain. **[3 marks]**

The auditory centre is found in the temporal lobe and its role is to process (i.e. decode) sounds. The sound vibrations enter the cochlea (in the inner ear), which converts sound waves to electrical nerve impulses. These nerve impulses travel to the brain stem, which decodes the sound in terms of duration, intensity, and frequency. The auditory information is then passed to the thalamus, which carries out further processing before the information is then passed to the auditory centre, where the sound is recognised and responded to if required.

Q43 Explain the role of Broca's area in the brain. **[3 marks]**

Broca's area is found in the frontal lobe of the brain and is found in the left hemisphere and is primarily responsible for speech production (speech sound). Broca's area is also considered to be responsible for controlling the movement of the muscles related to speaking (e.g. lips, tongue, larynx, and pharynx), which enable the processes of the articulation of sound.

Q44 Explain the role of Wernicke's area in the brain. **[3 marks]**

Wernicke's area is found in the posterior portion of the left temporal lobe, near the auditory cortex. The role of Wernicke's area is understanding language – the comprehension of speech. Information from the auditory centre is transferred to Wernicke's area, where it is recognised and understood as language.

Q45 Describe one study in which the localisation of brain function was investigated. Include details of what the psychologists did and what was found. **[3 marks]**

Peterson et al. (1988) used brain scans (PET and fMRI) to investigate the localisation of brain functions. The participants carried out either a cognitive task such as listening or a reading task. The researchers found in the images that Wernicke's area was active during a listening task and the Broca's area was active during a reading task, suggesting that some functions are localised.

Q46 Outline what research has shown about localisation of function in the brain.

WATCH OUT: *The word 'research' means theory/explanation and/or studies.*   **[3 marks]**

Research has shown hemispheric lateralisation of the brain, so the right hemisphere of the brain controls the left side of the body, and the left hemisphere controls the right side of the body. The right hemisphere of the brain is mainly concerned with visual and motor task functions. Research has also shown that some functions in the right hemisphere are more localised than others in the cortex. For example, the motor function (e.g. voluntary body movements and co-ordination) is mainly found in the frontal lobe of the brain, whereas the somatosensory cortex (which deals with sensations) is localised to the parietal lobe region. The left hemisphere of the brain is mainly concerned with visual and motor tasks functions. Research has shown the visual cortex (deals with our vision) is mainly located in the occipital lobe, and the auditory cortex (processes sounds) is found in the temporal lobe. Other functions, such as the language centre, seem more widely distributed on the left side of the hemisphere of the brain, but this is mainly located in the frontal lobe part of the brain. However, some aspects of language tend to be more localised. For example, the production of speech is localised to the Broca's area of the cortex, whereas the comprehension of speech is localised to the Wernicke's area of the frontal lobe.

Q47 Outline the nature of the motor centre in the brain.   **[3 marks]**

The motor centre is responsible for controlling and carrying out voluntary movements. The motor centre is located in the frontal lobe that runs across both cerebral hemispheres, with the centre on one side of the brain controlling the muscles on the opposite side of the body. Different parts of the motor centre control different parts of the body.

Application questions

Q48 Chris suffered a stroke to the left hemisphere of his brain, damaging Broca's area and the motor cortex.

Using your knowledge of the functions of Broca's area and the motor cortex, describe the problems that Chris is likely to experience.   **[3 marks]**

From the damage to Broca's area as a result of the stroke, Chris is likely to suffer from speech problems. This is known as Broca's aphasia. This means it will affect his language production but not his understanding. For example, Chris will only be able to talk in short meaningful sentences, which take great effort. He may find that his speech lacks fluency and have difficulty with certain words. As a consequence of damage to the motor cortex, Chris is likely to suffer from loss of muscle functions/ paralysis on the right side of the body. For example, loss of control or coordination of muscle movements.

Q49 Mira scored a high mark in her A-level English examination and claimed she has a 'left-sided brain'. 'You are talking nonsense', Damion says, 'you cannot have a left-sided brain. The whole brain works together to carry out functions.'

'It's not nonsense!' Mira replies. 'It says in my psychology textbook that the left brain is responsible for speech and language.'

Use your knowledge of localisation of function and/or hemisphere lateralisation to help understand Mira and Damion's discussion in your answer. Refer to Mira and Damion in your answer. **[6 marks]**

Mira believes she has a 'left-sided brain' because she is referring to the fact that Broca's area and the Wernicke's area are found in the left hemisphere of the brain and are considered to play a vital role in speech production and understanding language. In this respect, Mira is not 'talking nonsense', as the facts suggest that language is subject to hemispheric lateralisation, which means one hemisphere is dominated by the function of language. Research by Herasty (1997) found that women have proportionally larger Broca and Wernicke's areas than men, which can perhaps explain why she did so well in her A-level English examination and believes she has a more 'left-sided brain'.

Damion thinks she is 'talking nonsense' and believes that 'the whole brain works together to carry out functions'. His argument is in line with researchers who take a holistic approach and suggest that the production of language and understanding are too complex to be assigned to just one area and instead involve networks of brain regions. That is, the two hemispheres work together to form most tasks as part of a highly integrated system. Damion could be referring to the corpus callosum that enables information to be communicated between the two hemispheres.

Long-response questions

Q50 Discuss the extent to which the brain functions are localised. Refer to evidence in your answers. **[16 marks]**

Localisation of function in the brain refers to the idea that certain functions (e.g. movement, language, visual) tend to be in certain regions or specific areas in the brain (cerebral cortex). Before these discoveries (and the case of Phineas Gage), psychologists believed in a holistic theory that every single part of the brain was responsible for all thought and action. However, neuroimaging studies using brain scans (positron emission tomography (PET) and functional magnetic resonance imaging (fMRI)) have shown that some functions are more localised than others in the cortex.

Research has also shown hemispheric lateralisation of the brain, so the right hemisphere of the brain controls the left side of the body, and the left hemisphere controls the right side of the body. The right hemisphere of the brain is mainly concerned with visual-motor tasks (e.g. completing a dot-to-dot drawing). Research has shown that some functions in the right hemisphere are more localised than others in the cortex. For example, voluntary body movements and co-ordination functions are localised to the motor cortex area within the frontal lobe region of the brain, whereas the somatosensory cortex, which deals with sensations, is localised to the parietal lobe region of the brain. Research has shown that the visual cortex (which deals with our vision) is localised to the occipital lobe, and the auditory cortex (which processes sounds) is found in the temporal lobe.

The language function is more widely distributed on the left side of the hemisphere of the brain, but mainly in the frontal lobe of the brain. However, some aspects of language tend to be more localised. For example, the 'production of speech', is localised to the Broca's area of the frontal lobe. This discovery is based on case studies by Paul Broca on a number of patients with lesions (damage) in specific areas (inferior frontal gyrus), in the left frontal lobe area. Although these patients could understand spoken language, they had difficulties in producing speech, compared to patients with damage to these areas in the right hemisphere, who did not have the same language problems. The term Broca's aphasia is used today to describe patients who have difficulty in producing language (e.g. spoken or written) leading to slowness and lack of fluency.

It was Karl Wernicke, after a number of case studies, who identified a particular region in the frontal lobe of the left hemisphere, now known as the Wernicke's area, that is responsible for 'understanding language' (comprehension). He found that patients who did not have a problem in 'producing speech' but could not comprehend what was being said had damage to the Wernicke's area. The term Wernicke's aphasia is used today to describe patients who have difficulty in understanding spoken words.

There is research evidence to support the localisation theory. Peterson et al. (1988) used brain scans (PET and fMRI) to investigate the localisation of brain functions, especially for language and memory. The participants carried out either a cognitive task, such as listening, or a reading task. The researchers found evidence that showed Wernicke's area was active during a listening task and Broca's area was active during a reading task, suggesting that some functions are localised.

However, arguments against the localisation of function come from the evidence of plasticity. This is when the brain has become damaged through illness/accident, and a particular function has been compromised or lost, and the rest of the brain appears able to reorganise itself in an attempt to recover the lost function. Karl Lashley (1958) describes this as the equipotentiality theory, which states that if certain parts of the brain are damaged, other parts of the brain might take over the role of the damaged portion. According to this view, the effect of psychological or physiological damage on the brain is determined by the extent of damage to the brain rather than the location of the damage. This criticises Peterson et al's. (1998) study to some extent because it challenges the localisation theory, as it suggests that location is not important because the functions of the brain are carried out holistically, and even when damaged, other parts of the brain can compensate for this damage.

Those who support the holistic theory of the brain tend to reject the view that brain functions are localised. For example, the holistic theory of the brain states that all psychological and physiological functions are stored all over the brain. In 1950, Karl Lashley, a neuropsychologist, removed 10% to 50% of the cortex in rats that were learning a maze circuit. After this procedure, they were still able to perform the task without any problems. He concluded that the brain did not have any specific area for memory, and it appears to be stored all over. This is a criticism of the localisation theory as this shows that the idea of specific areas performing specific functions may not be completely accurate, which weakens the localisation theory. However, it could be argued there are physiological differences between rats and humans, and we should be cautious about generalising Lashley's findings to human beings.

This also supports the criticism that theories of localisation are biologically reductionist in nature and try to reduce very complex human behaviours and cognitive processes to specific regions of the brain. Such critics suggest that a more thorough understanding of the brain is required to truly understand complex cognitive processes like language.

In terms of language production, this may not be limited to Broca's area. Using brain MRI imaging, Dronkers et al. (2007) examined the preserved brains of two of Broca's patients, Louis Leborgne and Lazare Lelong, to identify the extent of the damage. The MRI scans revealed that both patients' lesions went significantly beyond the Broca region, and the lesions extended to other regions of the brain. The researchers concluded that the patients' aphasia (reduced speech abilities) may have been caused by the lesions just in the Broca's area alone, but also could be the result of damage to other neighbouring regions. This suggests that the production of language may involve a network of regions rather than being localised to specific areas.

Finally, some critics argue that the localisation theory fails to consider gender differences. For example, Herasty et al. (1997) found that women have larger Broca and Wernicke's areas than men, which may explain why women have more superior language skills than men. This study also suggests there is a level of beta bias in the localisation theory because the differences between men and woman in terms of variation of brain size and cognitive task performances tend to be ignored or not considered as important.

Split-brain research: hemispheric lateralisation

Identification questions

Q51 Complete the following sentence.

Circle one letter only. **[1 mark]**

Lateralisation means:

   A. The brain's ability to change and adapt to different and new experiences.

   B. Different hemispheres of the brain have different specialisms.

   C. Two halves of the brain are functionally the same.

   D. Surgical separation of the hemisphere of the brain.

Short-response questions

Q52 Explain what is meant by hemispheric lateralisation. **[3 marks]**

Hemispheric lateralisation refers to the fact that some physiological and mental processes in the brain are mainly specialised to either the left or right cerebral hemispheres. It also refers to the fact that the right hemisphere controls the left side of the body and the left visual field (left eye), and the left hemisphere controls the right side of the body and the right visual field (right eye).

Q53 Explain what is meant by split brain research. **[3 marks]**

Split-brain research refers to studies of patients who have been subjected to a surgical procedure called commissurotomy, which cuts the corpus callosum (nerve fibres) that connects the two hemispheres together. The purpose of split-brain research is to investigate the relationship between the two hemispheres and the extent to which brain functions are lateralised.

Q54 Split brain patients show unusual behaviour when tested in experiments. Briefly explain how unusual behaviour in split brain patients could be tested in an experiment. **[3 marks]**

One way to investigate behaviour in split brain patients is to carry out a split visual field experiment. Participants receive different visual stimuli (e.g. two different pictures). Each picture would only be visible to the left or to the right eye. The participants are then asked to verbally describe each picture they saw in their left and then their right eye.

Q55 Outline one research procedure used to investigate split-brain patients. **[3 marks]**

Split-brain research refers to studies of patients who have been subjected to a surgical procedure called commissurotomy, which cuts the corpus callosum (nerve fibres) that connects the two hemispheres together. The purpose of split-brain research is to investigate the relationship between the two hemispheres and the extent to which brain functions are lateralised.

Q56 Outline one research procedure used to investigate split-brain patients. **[6 marks]**

The split-brain procedure refers to patients who have been subjected to a surgical procedure called commissurotomy, which cuts the corpus callosum connecting the two hemispheres. The study by Sperry and Gazzaniga (1967) devised a number of visual and tactile (touch) tasks, setting separate tasks for each of the hemispheres. One visual task involved blindfolding one of the patient's eyes and then asking them to fixate with the other eye on a point (dot) in the middle of a screen. A visual stimulus (image e.g. chicken claw) was presented to the left or right-hand side of the fixation point on the screen and thus to the left or right visual field (eye). This was done at very high speed for less than 1/10 of a second, and the patient then had to describe what they saw. The presentation time was short to ensure that participants did not have enough time for eye movement, as this would 'spread' the information across both sides of the visual field, and therefore, across both sides of the brain. In the tactile test, an object was placed on the left or right. The patients could touch and feel the object, but they could not see their hands or what they were touching. Each time, the patient had to name and describe what they felt. Sperry recorded and analysed the behaviours to see whether the functions of the left and right hemispheres could be identified.

Q57 Briefly evaluate research using split brain patients to investigate hemispheric lateralisation of function. **[3 marks]**

There are methodological flaws in split-brain research investigating hemispheric lateralisation. For example, Sperry and Gazzaniga's (1967) experiment compared a group of 11 patients who all had a history of epileptic seizures and had undergone the split-brain procedure, with a control group with no history of epileptic seizures, who did not have the split-brain procedure.

It is argued that the control group cannot be considered a valid group for comparison, as we cannot rule out that the epilepsy of the 11 split-brain patients may have led to lateralisation. A more valid control group would have been people with a history of epilepsy, but who had not had the split-brain procedure, and in this way, we could determine if epilepsy led to lateralisation of certain brain regions.

Long-response questions

Q58 Outline and evaluate research into lateralisation and/or split-brain research.   **[16 marks]**

Brain lateralisation refers to the view that the left and the right parts of the brain control different physiological and mental functions. The right hemisphere controls and receives information from the left side of the body and the left hemisphere controls and receives information from the right side of the body. For example, the right hemisphere is mainly concerned with visual-motor tasks (e.g. a jigsaw puzzle), whereas the left hemisphere is mainly concerned with the production of language. The left and right hemispheres of the brain communicate with each other, mainly through a band of nerve fibres called the corpus callosum.

Split-brain research allows researchers a chance to investigate the different functional abilities of the two hemispheres, including the extent to which brain functions are lateralised. Split-brain research refers to studies of patients who have been subjected to a surgical procedure called commissurotomy, in which the corpus callosum has been cut. Sperry and Gazzaniga (1967) carried out experiments on hemispheric lateralisation on 11 split-brain patients (suffering from epilepsy) to test their functional capabilities. Normally, information from the left visual field goes to the right hemisphere, and information from the right visual field goes to the left hemisphere. Because the corpus callosum is cut in split-brain patients, the information presented to one hemisphere has no way of travelling to the other hemisphere, and therefore can only be processed in the hemisphere that received it.

Sperry and Gazzaniga's research confirmed the view that the two cerebral hemispheres are specialised for different functions. For example, if a split-brain patient was shown a picture of a cat in his right visual field (which sends that visual information to the left hemisphere), he could identify and describe the picture correctly. If the same picture was shown in the left visual field (which sends that information to the right hemisphere), the patient could not identify or describe the picture. This was because the visual information was processed in the right hemisphere. Then, it should have travelled over to the left hemisphere to the language centres, but this was not possible because the corpus callosum had been cut. This meant that the information remained in the right hemisphere, which had no language centres. In other words, the visual and language centres could not communicate with each other.

A strength of research into lateralisation is that it has shown us how lateralisation changes with normal ageing. Research has shown that lateralisation across many types of tasks and brain areas in younger individuals tends to switch to bilateral patterns (both hemispheres) in older adults. For example, Szaflarski et al. (2006) found that language became more lateralised to the left hemisphere with increasing age in children and adolescents, but after the age of 25, lateralisation decreased with age.

This might be because using the extra processing resources of the other hemisphere may in some way compensate for age-related decline in function.

The main advantage of humans having brain lateralisation appears to be an increase in neural processing capacity - the ability to carry out multiple tasks simultaneously. For example, Rogers (2004) found that in chickens, brain lateralisation is associated with an enhanced ability to perform two tasks simultaneously (e.g. finding food and being vigilant for predators). Using only one hemisphere to engage in a task leaves the other hemisphere free to engage in other functions. This provides evidence for the advantages of brain lateralisation because it enhances brain efficiency in cognitive tasks that demand the simultaneous but different use of both hemispheres. However, since this research was carried out on non-humans, caution is needed when applying the advantages of lateralised functioning from the chicken brain to the human brain.

A limitation of split-brain research is that the evidence is based on a very small sample of people, which makes generalisation on lateralisation more difficult to make. This is because the split-brain procedure is rare in the modern day, so there are limited numbers of 'split brain' patients available for such an investigation. Also, the 11 patients in Sperry's study all had a history of epileptic seizures.

This made the split-brain patients an unusual sample of people to test since epilepsy may have caused the unique changes in the brain, which could have influenced the findings in the study. Another criticism is that the control group in Sperry's study were people with no history of epileptic seizures and therefore potentially an inappropriate group to use as a comparison. A more appropriate control group would have been people with a history of epilepsy, who had not had the split-brain procedure. Therefore, we need to treat the findings from studies into hemispheric lateralisation with caution when generalising to the population, as they are based on a very small sample.

A further limitation is that some critics have argued that Sperry's split-brain study has overstated the differences in hemispheric function. Modern neuroscientists suggest that the actual distinction between each hemisphere is less clear and more complex. In a 'normal' brain, the two hemispheres are in constant communication when performing everyday tasks, and many of the behaviours typically associated with one hemisphere can be effectively performed by the other if the situation requires. For example, Turk et al. (2002) studied J.W, a patient who had suffered damage to the left hemisphere but eventually developed the capability to speak using the right hemisphere. This showed the brain's ability to adapt significantly following brain damage and suggested that lateralisation was not fixed.

Q59 Robert suffered a stroke at the age of 55. After the stroke, he was paralysed down his right side, though he could move his left arm and leg easily. Robert could clearly understand what was said to him but was unable to produce any speech.

Discuss how knowledge of hemispheric lateralisation and language centres in the brain has helped our understanding of cases such as Robert's. Refer to Robert's case in your answer.

[16 marks]

Hemispheric lateralisation is the view that the left and right parts of the brain control different physiological and psychological functions of the body. It also refers to the view that the right hemisphere (right side) of the brain controls and receives information from the left side of the body and the left visual field, and the left hemisphere (left side) of the brain controls and receives information from the right side of the body and the right visual field. Research has shown that the left hemisphere controls and processes the function of language and speech, whereas the right hemisphere controls motor functions (body movements). For example, Broca's area in the frontal lobe of the left hemisphere controls the 'production of speech', and Wernicke's area is responsible for 'comprehension - the interpretation of speech (understanding language). Damage to Broca's area leads to difficulty in the production of language (spoken or written), known as Broca's aphasia. Damage to Wernicke's area leads to difficulty in understanding language (spoken and written).

In the case of Robert, the right side of his body is paralysed, which supports hemisphere lateralisation. This is because Robert's stroke was localised in a certain area in the left hemisphere, which controls muscle movement to the right side of his body. Further evidence for hemispheric lateralisation is that Robert can 'clearly understand what was said to him' meaning that there is no damage to Wernicke's area in the left hemisphere from the stroke, and therefore he does not have Wernicke's aphasia. However, the fact that Robert is 'unable to produce any speech' can lead us to conclude that Broca's area has been damaged by the stroke, leading to Broca's aphasia.

There is research evidence to support hemispheric lateralisation. Sperry and Gazzaniga (1967) carried out experiments on hemispheric lateralisation on 11 split-brain patients suffering from epilepsy, whose corpus callosum had been cut, splitting the two hemispheres apart, which enabled the researchers to isolate each hemisphere and observe its function. They found that when a picture of an object (e.g. cat) was displayed to the right visual field of the patients, the patients could identify and describe what they saw. However, they could not identify or describe what they saw when the object was displayed to their left visual field. The findings demonstrate that the production of language is located mainly in the left hemisphere, because the patient should have been able to describe the object they saw in the left visual field (which they didn't), which goes to the right hemisphere of the brain. This study into lateralisation also helps explain cases like Robert's. The effect of the stroke can explain why Robert has lost the ability to speak properly and why he can move his left arm and legs but not his right side.

However, some critics have argued that Sperry's split-brain study has overstated the differences in hemispheric function. Modern neuroscientists suggest that the actual distinction between each hemisphere is less clear and more complex. In a 'normal' brain, the two hemispheres are in constant communication when performing everyday tasks, and many of the behaviours typically associated with one hemisphere can be effectively performed by the other when the situation requires. For example, Turk et al. (2002) studied J.W, a patient who had suffered damage to the left hemisphere but eventually developed the capability to speak using the right hemisphere. This showed the brain's ability to adapt significantly following brain damage and suggested that lateralisation was not fixed. This also suggests that Robert's inability to speak may be short-term, and over time he may recover his ability to speak.

One issue in researching hemispheric lateralisation is that the evidence is based on a very small sample of people, which makes generalisation on hemispheric lateralisation more difficult. This is because the split-brain procedure is rare in the modern day, so there are a limited number of 'split-brain' patients available for such an investigation. Also, the 11 patients in Sperry's all had a history of epileptic seizures. This made the split-brain patients an unusual sample of people to test since epilepsy may have caused the unique changes in the brain, which could have influenced the findings in the study.

Another criticism is that the control group in Sperry's study were people with no history of epileptic sseizures and therefore potentially an inappropriate group to use as a comparison. A more appropriate control group would have been people with a history of epilepsy, who had not had the split-brain procedure. We therefore need to treat the findings from studies into hemispheric lateralisation with caution when attempting to generalise the findings to the wider population, as they are based on a very small number of people.

A final criticism is that there is research evidence that lateralisation changes with age. For example, Szaflarski et al. (2006) found that language becomes more lateralised to the left hemisphere until the age of 25, although lateralisation then starts to decrease with age. Since Robert was 55 years of age when he had his stroke, his production of speech would have been less lateralised to the left hemisphere and possibly some language function is now also controlled by the right hemisphere, which may increase his chances of speech recovery.

Plasticity and functional recovery of the brain

Identification questions

Q60 What is the term that refers to the activation of a secondary neural pathway to carry out new brain function?

Circle one letter only. **[1 mark]**

    A. Synaptic Activation

    B. Masking

    C. Unmasking

    D. Neural initiation

Q61 What is the term that refers to the process where rarely used synapses in the brain are eliminated?

Circle one letter only. **[1 mark]**

    A. Synaptic pruning

    B. Synaptic unmasking

    C. Synaptic priming

    D. Synaptic degeneration

Short-response questions

Q62 Explain what is meant by plasticity in the brain. **[3 marks]**

Brain plasticity refers to the ability of the brain to change and adapt as a result of experiences. This means the brain continues to create new neural pathways and alter existing ones in response to experiences. The brain also appears to show evidence of functional recovery after a trauma (injury or disease) has occurred.

Q63 Outline research into functional recovery of the brain after trauma.

WATCH OUT: *The word 'research' means theory/explanation and/or studies. In this model answer we have focused on 'explanation' rather than studies.*

[6 marks]

The brain appears to show evidence of functional recovery after following a trauma, both structurally and functionally. This means that the brain's functions from a damaged area after trauma (injury or disease) are moved to another, undamaged area of the brain. For example, when a stroke damages brain cells, other parts sometimes take over their functions. The brain is able to 'rewire' itself by forming new synaptic connections. This can happen through a process called 'neural unmasking'. This is where dormant synapses (made inactive through low neural input) in the surrounding area of the damaged brain are activated or 'unmasked' by receiving more neural input, creating a lateral spread of activation. This, over time, leads to new secondary neural pathways (new circuits) being developed to compensate for the nearby damaged region. The brain has structurally reorganised itself to enable functional recovery.

Another way in which new neural pathways are created is by axonal sprouting. This is when undamaged axon cells grow new nerve endings to reconnect with neurons whose links were injured or severed. Undamaged axons can also sprout nerve endings and connect with other undamaged nerve cells, forming new neural pathways to accomplish a needed function.

Further structural change in the brain can occur through homologous area adaption. This is when damage to a particular region of the brain can be compensated for by shifting its function to the opposite side of the brain, often to the homologous (similar) side, in order to perform specific tasks. An example would be if Wernicke's area were damaged in the left hemisphere of the brain, the right-sided equivalent would take over the functions of the damaged area. The brain compensates for damage by reorganising and forming new connections between neurons, thus creating new neural pathways.

Q64 Outline research evidence for plasticity of the brain

WATCH OUT: *The word 'research' means theory/explanation and/or studies. In this model answer we have focused on 'explanation' rather than studies.*

[4 marks]

Maguire et al. (2000) found evidence for plasticity of the brain in taxi drivers. Using a magnetic resource imaging (MRI) scanner, he found significantly more volume of grey matter in the posterior hippocampus in London taxi drivers than in a matched control group (non-taxi drivers). This part of the brain is linked with the development of spatial and navigational skills. As part of their training, London cabbies take a complex test called 'The Knowledge' to assess their recall of city streets and possible routes. Their extensive learning experience of spatial navigation appears to alter the structure of the taxi drivers' brains. Maguire et al. found that the longer a person had spent as a taxi driver, the more pronounced the structural difference.

Application questions

Q65 Louise's grandad suffered a stroke to the left hemisphere, damaging Broca's area and the motor cortex. Louise is worried because she believes because of granddad's age, he will not be able to make any recovery.

Using your knowledge of plasticity and functional recovery of the brain after trauma, explain why Louise might be wrong. **[4 marks]**

Louise might be wrong that her grandad may not make a recovery because the functions that her granddad has lost (e.g. speech and movement in the right side) may transfer to other areas of his brain through the process of neuronal unmasking, leading to new secondary neural pathways (new circuits) to compensate for the damaged region. This would allow him to recover – over time – some of the functions that he has lost, despite his age, as research has shown that neural plasticity does continue throughout our lifespan. Furthermore, new experiences (e.g. physiotherapy) that increase brain stimulation of the opposite hemisphere may enhance plasticity, allowing his brain to change and adapt which may help him recover these lost functions.

Q66 Jemma is 10 years old. Last year she was involved in a serious accident and suffered injuries to her brain that caused problems with speech and understanding language. A year later, Jemma has recovered most of her language abilities.

Using your knowledge of plasticity and functional recovery of the brain after trauma, explain Jemma's recovery. **[4 marks]**

Research has shown that while the brain is still developing, recovery from trauma is more likely, explaining why Jemma has nearly made a full recovery. The functions that Jemma lost (e.g. producing and understanding speech) were transferred to other areas of her brain through the process of 'neuronal unmasking', leading to a new secondary neural pathway (new circuits) to compensate for the damaged area. Furthermore, new experiences (e.g. speech therapist/cognitive tasks) that increase brain stimulation of the opposite hemisphere may enhance plasticity, allowing her brain to change and adapt from the brain damage (e.g. swelling/haemorrhage) and recover more of these lost functions.

Long-response question

Q67 Describe and evaluate research into plasticity of the brain, including functional recovery after a trauma. **[16 marks]**

Brain plasticity refers to the ability of the brain to change and adapt as a result of experiences. This means the brain continues to create new neural pathways and alter existing ones in response to experiences. During infancy, the brain experiences rapid growth in the number of synaptic connections, peaking at around 15,000 at age 2–3 years (Gopnick et al., 1999).

As we age, connections that we rarely use get deleted and connections that we use a lot get strengthened. This process is known as synaptic pruning. It was once thought these changes were limited to childhood and that the adult brain would remain fixed. However, recent research suggests that neural connections can change or be formed at any time during a person's life. The brain is able to adapt to a changing environment constantly as a result of learning and new experiences.

Furthermore, the brain also appears to show evidence of functional recovery following a trauma, both structurally and functionally. This means that the brain's functions from a damaged area after trauma (injury or disease) are moved to another, undamaged area of the brain. For example, when a stroke damages brain cells, other parts sometimes take over their functions. The brain is able to 'rewire' itself by forming new synaptic connections. This can happen through a process called 'neural unmasking'. This is where dormant synapses (because low neural input has made them inactive) in the surrounding area of the damaged brain are activated or 'unmasked' by receiving more neural input than before, creating a lateral spread of activation. This, over time, leads to new secondary neural pathways (new circuits) being developed to compensate for the damaged region. The brain has structurally reorganised itself to enable functional recovery.

There are supporting research studies that demonstrate brain plasticity after exposure to an enriched environment. Maguire et al. (2000), using an MRI scanner, found significantly more volume of grey matter in the posterior hippocampus in London taxi drivers than in a matched control group (non-taxi drivers). This part of the brain is linked with the development of spatial and navigational skills. As part of their training, London cabbies take a complex test called 'The Knowledge' to assess their recall of city streets and possible routes. The taxi drivers' extensive learning experience of spatial navigation appears to alter the structure of their brains. Maguire et al. found that the longer a person had spent as a taxi driver, the more pronounced the structural difference.

Another strength is that research into plasticity and functional recovery has practical applications in real life. For example, our increased understanding in this area has contributed to the field of neurorehabilitation – the treatment of those who have suffered brain trauma. Techniques include the use of motor therapy and electrical stimulation of the brain to counter the reduced cognitive functions following a brain injury (e.g. a stroke.) Although the brain can fix itself to a certain extent, some intervention may be needed if there is to be a full recovery. This shows that research into plasticity and functional recovery has improved people's quality of life because rehabilitation programmes based on such research have been shown to work.

A limitation of neural plasticity is that it can sometimes have negative consequences. The brain's ability to rewire itself can have maladaptive behavioural consequences. For example, prolonged drug use has been shown to result in poorer cognitive functioning and an increased risk of dementia in later life (Medina et al., 2007). Also, 60-80% of amputees develop 'phantom limb' syndrome (the continuing experience of sensation in the missing limb as if it were still there), which is usually painful and thought to be due to reorganisation in the somatosensory cortex (Ramachandran and Hirstein, 1998). This evidence suggests that structural and physical processes involved in functional recovery may not always be beneficial and can lead to unpleasant and painful experiences.

Another limitation is that the relationship between age and functional plasticity is complex, making it difficult to understand. It is known that plasticity also tends to reduce with age, making the brain less able to recover functions following a trauma. For example, Marquez de la Plata et al. (2008) found that after brain trauma, older patients (40+ years old) regained less function in treatment than younger patients. However, Bezzola et al. (2012) used functional magnetic resonance imaging (fMRI) scans to show that 40 hours of golf training increased neural representation of movement in areas of the motor cortex in middle-aged participants (40-60 years), compared to a control group (no golf training). This shows that neural plasticity does continue throughout our lifespan.

A further limitation of plasticity and functional recovery is that it depends on several variables. The brain's ability to recover will vary according to the extent and location of the damage and the individual. The more extensive the damage, the less likely recovery will be. A person's level of educational attainment will also influence how well the brain recovers after trauma. Schneider et al. (2014) retrospectively examined data from the US Traumatic Brain Injury Systems Database and found nearly 40% of patients with a college-level education achieved 'disability-free' recovery within a year after a moderate-to-severe traumatic brain injury, compared with less than 10% of patients who left school early. The researchers concluded that 'cognitive reserve' could be a factor in neural adaptation during recovery from traumatic brain injury. This suggests that individual differences vary extensively between patients, which makes it difficult to generalise plasticity and functional recovery.

Ways of studying the brain

Identification questions

Q68 Which of the following, A, B, C, or D, is a feature of functional magnetic resonance imaging?

Circle one letter only. **[1 mark]**

A. Indirectly measuring the electrical activity of neurons by recording changes in neurotransmitter release.

B. Indirectly measuring the electrical activity of neurons by recording changes in brain blood flow.

C. Directly measuring the electrical activity of neurons using electrodes on the scalp.

D. Directly measuring the electrical activity of neurons using electrodes implanted in the brain.

Q69 Which method of studying the brain would most accurately identify specific brain areas activated during a cognitive task?

Circle one letter only. **[1 mark]**

A. Event-related potentials (ERPs)

B. Functional magnetic resonance imaging (fMRI)

C. Event-related potentials (ERPs)

D. Electroencephalogram (EEGs)

Short-response questions

Q70 Outline electroencephalograms (EEGs) as a way of studying the brain. **[4 marks]**

An electroencephalogram (EEG) is a machine that measures electrical activity in the brain when a skull cap with electrodes is placed on a person's head. The EEG machine detects 'brainwaves', which are electrical neurons communicating with each other as a result of activity in the brain. The EEG machine records the brainwave patterns generated from millions of neurons, which show overall brain activity. There are four basic EEG wave patterns: alpha waves, beta waves, delta waves and theta waves. The EEG is often used as a diagnostic tool; for example, unusual arrhythmic wave patterns of brain activity may indicate abnormalities such as epilepsy, sleep disorders or dementia.

Q71 Outline one strength and one limitation of electroencephalograms (EEGs). **[4 marks]**

One strength of the electroencephalogram (EEG) technique is that it provides valuable information about brain activity. For example, it helps us to understand the different stages of a sleep cycle. It is also a valuable diagnostic tool for certain brain abnormalities such as epilepsy.

One limitation of EEGs is that the electrodes on the skull cap can only detect the activity in superficial regions of the brain but cannot reveal what is going on in the deeper regions, such as the hypothalamus or hippocampus.

Q72 Outline event-related potentials (ERPs) as a way of studying the brain. **[4 marks]**

Event-related potentials (ERPs) are the measurable responses of the brain (brainwave activity), which are the direct result of a specific stimulus task (e.g. looking at an image or doing mental arithmetic). ERPs can be measured by an electroencephalogram (EEG) by placing a skull cap with electrodes on the person's scalp. In the ERP technique, the same stimuli are presented repeatedly to see which part of the brain is particularly active compared to other background brain activity. The ERP technique uses a computer program that 'averages out' the responses so that the most common stimulus-related brain activity remains, and the irrelevant background brainwave activity is cancelled, leaving a clear signal – the event-related potential neurons.

Q73 Outline one strength and one limitation of event-related potentials (ERPs). **[4 marks]**

One strength of the event-related potential (ERP) technique is that it provides useful information about the precise timing of brain-processing activity in response to a stimulus. For example, psychologists can precisely measure the time response for certain cognitive tasks (e.g. describing an images or shape) to influence speech production.

One limitation of ERPs is their poor spatial resolution (the image display of the location). This means we cannot use them to establish the precise brain region associated with the performance of any given tasks and thus only allow estimations.

Q74 Outline functional magnetic resonance imaging (fMRI) as a way of studying the brain.

[4 marks]

Functional magnetic resonance imaging (fMRI) is a technique that detects and measures changes in brain activity while a person performs a task (e.g. movement, reading, etc.). It does this by measuring changes in blood flow in areas of the brain. An increase in blood flow indicates neural activity in those areas. The fMRI produces moving visual images (known as 'activation maps') showing changes in blood flow, demonstrating that this part of the brain is involved in a particular mental activity. fMRI may be used to detect and examine the localisation of the brain (e.g. determine which parts of the brain perform certain functions or evaluate the effects of a stroke or other disease on brain function).

Q75 Outline one strength and one limitation of functional magnetic resonance imaging (fMRI).

[4 marks]

One strength of functional magnetic resonance imaging (fMRI) is that it is non-invasive. This is because it does not involve the insertion of instruments into the body, and it does not expose the brain to potentially harmful radiation, as is the case with some other scanning techniques used in the study of the brain, such as positron emission tomography (PET).

One limitation of fMRI is that it can only measure changes in blood flow in the brain. This means it cannot directly measure neural activity in particular brain areas, and therefore only provides an indirect measure of neural activity. This means we cannot be sure if a cognitive task, for example, actually caused the physiological changes in brain activity.

Q76 Outline the post-mortem examination as a way of studying the brain.　　　**[4 marks]**

Post-mortem examinations involve examining a person's brain after they have died. Anatomical areas of the brain are examined to try and link abnormalities in the brain to explain certain behaviours during the person's lifetime and to establish the likely cause of a disorder the person suffered. This may also involve comparing the dead person's brain with a neurotypical brain (normal brain), in order to assess the difference. Post-mortem studies have also been used to establish a link between psychological disorders, such as schizophrenia, and underlying brain abnormalities.

Q77 Outline one strength and one limitation of post-mortem examination.　　　**[4 marks]**

One strength of post-mortem examinations is that they allow for a more detailed examination of the anatomy of the brain than would be possible with the sole use of non-invasive scanning techniques, such as functional magnetic resonance imaging (fMRI) and electroencephalograms (EEGs). For example, post-mortem examinations enable researchers to examine deeper regions of the brain, such as the hypothalamus and the hippocampus, and gain a much better understanding of certain brain abnormalities (e.g. schizophrenia, language as identified by Broca and Wernicke).

One limitation of the post-mortem examination is the interpretation of the results. The discovery of a damaged/abnormal brain is often used to explain the associated disorder the patient was suffering from. However, this may not have been the cause of the psychological disorder. The brain abnormality may have been caused by some other trauma or decay, for example, prolonged drug usage.

Q78 The electroencephalogram (EEG) and event-related potentials (ERPs) both involve recording the electrical activity of the brain.

Outline one difference between the EEG and ERP. **[2 marks]**

The electroencephalogram (EEG) is a recording of general brain activity, usually linked to states such as sleep and arousal, whereas event-related potentials (ERPs) are a measure of brain activity as a result of a specific stimulus presented to the participant.

Long-response questions

Q79 Describe and evaluate scanning techniques as a way of studying the brain. **[16 marks]**

One scanning technique is functional magnetic resonance imaging (fMRI), which measures changes in brain activity while a person performs a task (e.g. movement, reading, etc.). It does this by measuring the increase in changes in blood flow areas of the brain, which indicates increased neural activity in those areas. As a result of these changes in blood flow, researchers are able to produce moving visual images (known as 'activation maps'), showing which areas of the brain are involved in a particular mental activity. fMRI may be used to detect and examine the localisation of the brain, for example, to determine which parts of the brain are handling critical functions, evaluate the effects of a stroke or other disease, or to guide brain treatment.

A strength of fMRI is that it is non-invasive. This is because it does not involve the insertion of instruments into the body, and it does not expose the brain to potentially harmful radiation, as is the case with some other scanning techniques used in the study of the brain, such as positron emission tomography (PET). This is a strength because it allows more patients to undertake fMRI scans, which could help psychologists to understand more about the functioning of the human brain, which in turn will deepen our understanding of its localisation function. However, a limitation of fMRI is that it can only measure changes in blood flow in the brain. This means it cannot directly measure neural activity in particular brain areas, and therefore only provides an indirect measure of neural activity. This means we cannot be sure if a cognitive task, for example, caused the physiological changes in brain activity.

The electroencephalogram (EEG) is another scanning technique that measures electrical activity within the brain when a skull cap with electrodes is placed on a person's head. The EEG machine detects 'brainwaves', which are electrical neurons communicating with each other as a result of activity in the brain. The EEG machine records the brainwave patterns generated from millions of neurons, which shows overall brain activity. The four basic EEG patterns are alpha waves, beta waves, delta waves and theta waves. The EEG is often used as a diagnostic tool. For example, unusual arrhythmic wave patterns of brain activity may indicate abnormalities such as epilepsy, sleep disorders and dementia.

A strength of the EEG technique is that it provides valuable information about brain activity. For example, it is a valuable tool for diagnosing certain disorders such as epilepsy, as well as providing valuable understanding of the different stages of sleep. However, a limitation of EEGs is that they can only detect the activity in superficial regions of the brain but cannot reveal what is going on in the deeper regions, such as the hypothalamus or hippocampus.

Event-related potentials (ERPs) are measurable responses of the brain (brainwave activity) created by very small voltage changes as a result of a specific stimulus (e.g. sensory, cognitive or motor task) presented to the participant. ERPs are also measured by an EEG) by placing a skull cap with electrodes on the person's scalp. Psychologists use ERPs to investigate the neural activity of certain cognitive processes, e.g. attention, language, and memory.

A strength of the ERP technique is that it provides useful information about the precise timing of brain processing activity in response to a stimulus. For example, psychologists can precisely measure the time response for certain cognitive tasks (images or shapes) to influence speech production. However, a limitation of ERPs is their poor spatial resolution (the image display of the location). This means we cannot use them to establish the precise brain region associated with the performance of any given tasks and thus can only provide estimations.

Post-mortem examinations involve examining a person's brain after they have died. Anatomical areas of the brain are examined to try and link abnormalities in their brain to explain certain behaviours during their lifetime and to establish the likely cause of a disorder the person suffered.

This may also involve comparing the dead person's brain with a neurotypical brain (normal brain) to assess the extent of the difference. Post-mortem studies have also been used to establish a link between psychological disorders such as schizophrenia and underlying brain abnormalities.

A strength of post-mortem examinations is that they allow for a more detailed examination of anatomical of the brain than would be possible with the sole use of non-invasive scanning techniques, such as fMRI and EEG. For example, it enables researchers to examine deeper regions of the brain, such as the hypothalamus and the hippocampus and a much better understanding of certain brain abnormalities (e.g. schizophrenia, language as identified by Broca and Wernicke). However, one limitation of the post-mortem examination is the interpretation of the results. The discovery of a damaged/abnormal brain is often used to explain the associated disorder the patient was suffering from. However, this may not have been the cause, and the behaviour disorder may have been caused by some other related trauma or decay. For example, brain abnormality could have been caused by prolonged drug usage.

Q80 Describe and evaluate one or more ways of studying the brain.   **[16 marks]**

One scanning technique is functional magnetic resonance imaging (fMRI), which measures changes in brain activity while a person performs a task (e.g. movement, reading, etc.). It does this by measuring the changes in blood flow in areas of the brain. When the brain's nerve cells are more active, red blood cells consume more glucose and oxygen, and this leads to a local increase in blood flow in that particular area, which indicates increased neural activity. As a result of these changes in blood flow, researchers can produce a dynamic moving picture of the brain (known as an 'activation map'), showing which areas of the brain are involved in a particular mental activity. fMRI may be used to detect and examine the localisation of the brain, for example to determine which parts of the brain are handling critical functions, evaluate the effects of a stroke or other disease, or to guide brain treatment.

A strength of fMRI is that it is non-invasive. This is because it does not involve the insertion of instruments into the body, and it does not expose the brain to potentially harmful radiation, as is the case with some other scanning techniques used in the study of the brain, such as positron emission tomography (PET). The fact that fMRI is virtually risk-free is a strength because it allows more patients to undertake fMRI scans, which could help psychologists to understand more about the functioning of the human brain, thus deepening our understanding of its localisation of function.

Another strength of fMRI is that it can provide a moving picture of the whole brain's activity. This means that fMRI can not only capture active localised brain activity (mind mapping); it can also capture the entire network of the brain areas that are engaged when subjects undertake tasks. This is something that other methods such as MRI/post-mortem examinations cannot do since they simply show the physiological structure of the brain. This is a strength because this technique can show which areas in the brain are actively involved in activities done by the person. However, an fMRI only tells you that a region is active during a process, not that it is necessary for a process.

A limitation of fMRI is that it can only measure changes in blood flow in the brain. This means it cannot directly measure neural activity in particular brain areas, and therefore only provides an indirect measure of neural activity. This means we cannot be sure if a cognitive task caused the physiological changes in brain activity. Another limitation of fMRI is that it is expensive. fMRI machines are expensive to buy and maintain compared to other techniques. This makes research expensive and difficult to organise. A single MRI scan can cost around £2,000. The high cost of fMRI research means that sample sizes are small due to the limited availability of funding. The cost per participant is high. The sample size negatively impacts the validity of the research, making it difficult to generalise.

The electroencephalogram (EEG) is another scanning technique that measures electrical activity within the brain when electrodes are placed on a skull cap on a participant's head. Different numbers of electrodes can be used, depending on the focus of the research. The EEG machine detects 'brainwaves', which are created by electrical neurons as a result of activity in the brain. The EEG machine records the brainwave patterns generated from millions of neurons and these patterns overall brain activity. The four basic EEG patterns are alpha waves, beta waves, delta waves and theta waves. The EEG is often used as a diagnostic tool, for example, unusual arrhythmic wave patterns of brain activity may indicate abnormalities such as epilepsy, sleep disorders or dementia.

A strength of the EEG technique is that it provides valuable information about brain activity. For example, the EEG is a valuable tool for diagnosing certain disorders such as epilepsy, as well as providing a valuable understanding of the different stages of sleep, which has deepened our knowledge of circadian rhythms. Another strength of EEGs is that they are cheaper than fMRI. This means that EEGs are more widely available to researchers, and since they are non-invasive, they present no risk to participants. This is a strength because the relatively low cost of EEGs means that larger sample sizes can be used in research and therefore, we can generalise from the research findings.

However, a limitation of EEGs is that they can only detect the activity in superficial regions of the brain but cannot reveal what is going on in the deeper regions, such as the hypothalamus or hippocampus, and therefore this limits our understanding of brain activity at least for certain regions.

Another issue with EEGs is their poor spatial resolution (the image display of the location). This is because the electrical neuronal activity is generated several centimetres below the recording scalp electrodes. The electrical neuronal activity must go through various resistive layers in the skull, which means that once the activity reaches the scalp electrodes, it provides a blurred view. This is a limitation when using EEGs because we cannot provide accurate information about neural activities because of the poor spatial resolution. This means we cannot use them to establish the precise brain region activities associated with the performance of any given task.

Biological rhythms

Identification question

Q81 Which of the following is an example of a circadian rhythm?

Circle one letter only. **[1 mark]**

    A. The five stages of sleep

    B. The menstrual cycle

    C. The sleep/wake cycle

    D. Body temperature

    E. Seasonal affective disorder

Short-response questions

Q82 Explain what is meant by circadian. **[2 marks]**

A circadian rhythm is a biological rhythm in our body that repeats itself approximately every 24 hours. An example of a circadian rhythm is the sleep/wake cycle.

Q83 Outline one example of a circadian rhythm. **[2 marks]**

An example of a circadian rhythm is the sleep/wake cycle behaviour. Our circadian rhythm is controlled by endogenous pacemakers, which are our internal biological 'clocks'. The master circadian pacemaker is called the suprachiasmatic nucleus (SCN). The SCN, which controls our circadian rhythm, is also influenced by exogenous 'zeitgebers', environmental cues such as light. Exogenous zeitgebers help set the sleep/wake cycle so that the body is in synchrony with the outside world.

Q84 Describe one study into circadian rhythms. In your answer explain what the researcher(s) did and what they found. **[4 marks]**

Michel Siffre (1975) subjected himself to two months living underground in a cave to study his own circadian rhythms. While living underground, he was deprived of external cues to guide his circadian rhythms, e.g. no daylight, clocks, or the radio; and he woke, ate and slept when he felt it was appropriate to do so.

The only thing influencing his behaviour was the 'free-running' circadian rhythm of his internal body clock. Siffre found that his natural circadian rhythm was slightly longer from the usual 24 hours to around 25 hours, but he did have regular sleep/wake cycles. This suggests that the internal control (endogenous pacemaker) of the circadian rhythm can maintain a regular daily cycle, even when there are no external cues.

Long-response questions

Q85 Outline and evaluate circadian rhythms. **[16 marks]**

The circadian rhythm is a biological rhythm in our body that repeats itself approximately every 24 hours. An example of a circadian rhythm is the sleep/wake cycle behaviour. Our circadian rhythm is regulated by endogenous pacemakers, which are biological 'clocks' that are found in all cells, tissues or organs (referred to as peripheral circadian oscillators). The clocks are controlled and synchronised to work together by a master circadian pacemaker (master clock) called the suprachiasmatic nucleus (SCN), which is in the hypothalamus. The SCN has been identified as controlling our sleep-waking cycle. The SCN is also influenced by external cues in the environment known as exogenous 'zeitgebers'. The most important exogenous zeitgeber is light, which is responsible for resetting the body clock each day and keeping it on a 24-hour cycle, so that the body is in synchrony with the outside world.

In terms of the sleep/wake cycle, the circadian rhythm not only dictates when we should be asleep but also when we should be awake. Exogenous zeitgebers, such as light and dark, are the external signals for when we sleep and when we wake up. Light is first detected by the eye, which then sends messages concerning the level of brightness to the suprachiasmatic nuclei (SCN). The SCN then uses this information to co-ordinate the activity of the entire circadian system. Sleeping and wakefulness are not determined by the circadian rhythm alone but also under the control of the homoeostasis (body's regulation) mechanism. Homeostasis tells the body when the need for sleep is increasing, depending on the amount of energy consumed during the day in an awake state. This homeostatic drive for sleep increases throughout the day, reaching its maximum in the late evening when most people fall asleep.

Research has shown that circadian sleep/wake cycles can vary between people. Czeisler et al. (1999) examined circadian cycles and found that they can vary from 13 to 65 hours. Also, people appear to be innately different in terms of when their circadian rhythms peak. Duffy et al. (2001) found that 'morning people' prefer to rise and go to bed early (about 6 am and 10 pm) whereas 'evening people' prefer to wake and go to bed later (10 am and 1 am).

There is supporting research that provides evidence for circadian rhythms and the effect external cues have on our cycle. Michel Siffre (1975) subjected himself to two months living underground in a cave to study his own circadian rhythms. While living underground, he was deprived of external cues to guide his circadian rhythms, e.g. no daylight, clocks, or the radio; and he woke, ate and slept when he felt it was appropriate to do so. The only thing influencing his behaviour was the 'free-running' circadian rhythm of his internal body clock. Siffre found that his natural circadian rhythm was slightly longer (around 25 hours), but he did have regular sleep/wake cycles. This suggests that the internal control (endogenous pacemaker) of the circadian rhythm, can maintain a regular daily cycle, even when there are no external cues (exogenous zeitgebers).

However, a limitation is that there is poor control in the research studies that investigate circadian rhythm. Participants deprived of natural light in the studies often still had access to artificial light. For example, Siffre had a lamp turned on from when he woke up until he went to bed, assuming artificial light would not affect free-running circadian rhythms. However, another study suggests that this is not true. Czeisler et al. (1999) adjusted participants' circadian rhythms from 22 to 28 hours by using dim artificial lighting alone. This finding shows that circadian rhythms are affected by artificial light and that researchers may have ignored an important confounding variable in circadian rhythm research.

A further limitation of research into circadian rhythms is further methodological issues. The sleep/wake studies tend to use only small groups of participants (or a single person, e.g. Siffre). We therefore need to be cautious about generalising because the people involved may not be representative of the wider population. Siffre's most recent study showed that his internal body clock was much slower as a 60-year-old man, than it was in his younger days. This suggests that, even when the same person is involved, there are factors that may prevent general conclusions from being drawn.

Despite the above limitations, circadian rhythm research does have strengths in that it has a practical application to shift work. For example, Boivin et al. (1996) found that shift workers experience a lapse of concentration around 6 am (a circadian trough), so mistakes and accidents are more likely at that time. Research also suggests a link between shift work and poor health, with shift workers three times more likely to develop heart disease (Knutsson, 2003). Thus, research into the sleep/wake cycle may have economic implications in terms of how best to manage worker productivity.

Although studies have shown 'light' as being the most important exogenous zeitgeber influencing the SCN, other psychologists have questioned this. For example, Buhr et al. (2010) believed it is temperature rather than light that controls our circadian sleep/wake cycle. Buhr et al. claimed that light levels may trigger the suprachiasmatic nuclei (SCN), but the SCN then transforms the light levels into neural messages that set the body's temperature. Buhr found that these fluctuations in body temperature set the timing of cells in the body, and therefore cause tissues and organs to become active or inactive. This suggests more research is needed to fully understand the nature of exogenous zeitgebers and the effect they have on the circadian rhythm.

Infradian and ultradian rhythms

Identification questions

Q86 The human female menstrual cycle is an example of one type of biological rhythm, known as a:

Circle one letter only. **[1 mark]**

    A. Circadian rhythm.

    B. Infradian rhythm.

    C. Ultradian rhythm.

Q87 Which two are examples of infradian rhythms?

Circle two letters only. **[2 marks]**

    A. Stages of sleep

    B. The menstrual cycle

    C. The sleep/wake cycle

    D. Seasonal affective disorder

Q88 Which is an example of ultradian rhythms?

Circle one letter only. **[1 mark]**

    A. Stages of sleep

    B. The menstrual cycle

    C. The sleep/wake cycle

    D. Seasonal affective disorder

Short-response questions

Q89   Using an example, explain what is meant by the term 'infradian rhythms'.   **[4 marks]**

Infradian rhythms are repeating biological cycles that last for more than 24 hours (more than a day). They can be weekly, monthly, seasonal, or annual cycles. One example is the female menstruation cycle, which happens on a monthly cycle. There are considerable variations in the length of this cycle, with some women having a short 23-day cycle and others having a cycle as long as 36 days, with the average around 28 days.

Q90   Using an example, explain what is meant by the term 'ultradian rhythms'.   **[3 marks]**

Ultradian rhythms are repeating biological cycles that have a duration of less than 24 hours (less than a day). One example is the five stages of sleep that make up a typical night's sleep. The ultradian rhythm found in human sleep follows a pattern of alternating rapid eye movement (REM) and non-rapid eye movement (NREM) sleep. This cycle repeats itself about every 90–100 minutes throughout the night. A person can experience up to five full sleep cycles in a night.

Q91   Outline research into infradian rhythms.   **[3 marks]**

Stern and McClintock (1998) wanted to show that the menstrual cycle is not totally regulated by the internal biological clock (endogenous pacemaker) of the hypothalamus. Samples of pheromones (chemicals secreted during sweat) were collected from 29 females with irregular menstrual cycles. Pheromones were collected using cotton pads, which nine of the women wore under their armpits for a minimum of eight hours at different stages of their menstruation cycles. These pads were cleaned with alcohol and later rubbed on the upper lips of the other 20 females and then their menstrual cycles were monitored over a period of time. They found that 68% of women experienced changes to their cycle that brought them closer in timing to the cycle of the 'pheromones donor'. This research shows that infradian rhythms, such as the menstruation cycle, can be affected by external factors (zeitgebers), in this case, pheromones. This may explain why when a group of women live in close proximity, their menstrual cycles tend to synchronise.

Q92 Outline research into ultradian rhythms.

WATCH OUT: In this answer we have not used a study but given an explanation/theory instead. Remember, the word 'research' can mean studies and/or theory. We have used stages of sleep as an example for 'ultradian rhythm'. Remember, the focus needs to be rhythmic pattern of the sleep stages rather than describing in too much detail the stages of REM and NREM sleep.
[6 marks]

Researchers have investigated human sleep patterns as an example of an ultradian rhythm. Researchers using electroencephalographs (EEGs) to look at electrical brainwave activity have shown that human sleep follows a rhythmic pattern throughout the night. In an average night's sleep, a person will go through five cycles of sleep, rather than just one long period of sleep.

These alternating cycles are made up of non-rapid eye movement (NREM) and rapid eye movement (REM) sleep. NREM consists of stages 1-to-4 in the sleep cycle and REM is the fifth stage. In each stage, the EEG shows different brain activity. In the first four stages (NREM), brainwave activity slows down as you progress through the stages. In the fifth stage (REM), brainwave activity speeds up and resembles that of a person being awake. This cycle repeats itself about every 90–100 minutes throughout the night in a rhythmic pattern. A person can experience up to five full sleep cycles in a night.

Long-response questions

Q93 Outline and evaluate infradian rhythms and/or ultradian rhythms. **[16 marks]**

Infradian rhythms are repeating biological cycles that last for more than 24 hours (more than a day). They can be weekly, monthly, seasonal, or annual cycles. One example is the female menstruation cycle, which happens on a monthly cycle and is regulated by the endogenous pacemaker (the body's internal biological clock) in the hypothalamus. The hypothalamus causes the pituitary gland to produce certain chemicals that are important in determining the menstrual cycle. These hormones promote ovulation (release of an egg) and stimulate the uterus for fertilisation (thickening of the womb lining with nutrients and blood) to prepare for pregnancy. After two weeks, if there is no fertilisation, the uterine lining breaks down, which leads to menstruation. There are considerable variations in the length of this cycle, with some women having short 23-day cycles and others having a cycle as long as 36 days, with the average around 28 days.

Ultradian rhythms are repeating biological cycles that have a duration of less than 24 hours (less than a day). One example is the sleep cycle, which has five stages. Researchers using electroencephalographs (EEGs) to look at electrical brainwave activity have shown that human sleep follows a rhythmic pattern of stages and cycles throughout the night. In an average night's sleep, a person can experience up to five full cycles of sleep, rather than just one long period of sleep. Each cycle comprises five stages of non-rapid eye movement (NREM) and rapid eye movement (REM) sleep. NREM consists of stages 1-to-4 in the cycle of sleep and REM is the fifth stage. In each stage, the EEG shows different brain activity. In the first four stages (NREM), brainwave activity slows down as you progress through the stages. In the fifth stage (REM), brainwave activity speeds up and resembles that of a person being awake and is the stage where dreaming occurs. The sleep cycle repeats about every 90–100 minutes throughout the night in a rhythmic pattern.

There is research evidence to support the view that the menstrual cycle can also be controlled by exogenous cues. Stern and McClintock (1998) wanted to show that the menstrual cycle is not totally regulated by the internal biological clock of the hypothalamus. A sample of 29 females with irregular menstrual cycles were selected. Pheromones (chemicals secreted during sweat) were collected using cotton pads, which nine of the women wore under their armpits for a minimum of eight hours at different stages of their menstruation cycles. These pads were then cleaned with alcohol and later rubbed on the upper lips of the other 20 females and their menstrual cycles were monitored over a period of time. They found that 68% of women experienced changes to their cycle that brought them closer in timing to the cycle of the 'pheromones donor'. This shows that infradian rhythms, such as the menstruation cycle, can be affected by external factors (zeitgebers), in this case, pheromones. This may explain why when a group of women live in close proximity; their menstrual cycles tend to synchronise.

A limitation of studies into menstruation synchrony, as above, is that there are methodological issues. There may be confounding variables involved in the research which have not been considered. There are many factors that may influence the timing of a woman's menstrual cycle, such as stress, changes in diet and exercise. Therefore, any pattern of the synchronisation effect demonstrated by Stern and McClintock's study may have occurred by chance. Also, the study involved a small sample of women, and it relied on them self-reporting the onset of their own cycle, which may be inaccurate. As a result, external factors (zeitgebers) such as pheromones may not have much impact on the menstrual cycle of a woman, as the research evidence may not be valid.

There is research to support the different stages in sleep. Dement and Kleitman (1957) recorded the EEG sleep patterns of nine adults in a sleep laboratory. The researchers were able to wake the participants during each of the different stages of sleep. The participants were asked to report their feelings, experiences and emotions. The researchers found that people awakened during the REM sleep stage reported dreams 80-90% of the time and reported an accurate recall of their dreams. The study suggests that REM (dreaming) sleep is a distinct ultradian rhythm and this supports the different stages of the ultradian sleep cycle.

There is evidence to show that differences in people's sleeping patterns, e.g. how many hours of sleep or time taken to sleep, may not be due to social factors, e.g. lifestyle, habit, temperature, as it is often suggested. For example, Tucker et al. (2007) asked a sample of 21 participants to spend eight nights in a controlled laboratory environment and found large differences between their sleeping patterns, such as sleep duration, time to fall asleep, and the amount of time in each sleep stage (stages 1 through 4 and REM sleep). This study suggests that the differences between participants were not driven by their circumstances but were largely biologically determined, possibly genetic in origin.

Endogenous pacemakers and exogenous zeitgebers

Short-response questions

Q94 Explain what is meant by an endogenous pacemaker. **[2 marks]**

Endogenous pacemakers are our internal biological 'clocks' that regulate our internal biological rhythms. The suprachiasmatic nucleus (SCN) is the main endogenous pacemaker and acts as a 'master' clock. It has been identified as controlling our sleep/waking cycle and synchronising all the other biological clocks throughout our body.

Q95 Explain what is meant by an exogenous zeitgeber. **[2 marks]**

Exogenous zeitgebers are environmental cues, such as light, that help to regulate and reset our biological clocks, such as the sleep/wake cycle.

Q96 Describe one study that investigated the effects of endogenous pacemakers on the sleep/wake cycle. **[6 marks]**

The effects of endogenous pacemaker have been demonstrated in animal studies. Morgan (1995) conducted research by breeding mutant hamsters so that they had an abnormal sleep/wake cycle of 20 hours rather than 24 hours. The suprachiasmatic nucleus (SCN) neurons from these abnormal hamsters were transplanted into the brains of normal hamsters, and as a result, displayed the same sleep/wake cycle of 20 hours. In a follow-up experiment, the SCN neurons from the normal hamster with a 24-hour sleep cycle were transplanted into the brains of the abnormal hamsters, which resulted in their abnormal 20-hour circadian rhythm changing to a 24-hour rhythm. This research shows the importance of SCN as an endogenous pacemaker in governing the body's sleep/wake cycle.

Q97 Describe one study that investigated the effects of an endogenous zeitgeber on the sleep/wake cycle. **[6 marks]**

Campbell and Murphy (1998) carried out a study to see the effect of light on the sleep/wake cycle. The experiment involved 15 volunteers who slept in a laboratory for four days and nights. The researchers woke the participants at various times (2 pm, 9 am, 4 am, etc.), and shone a bright light onto the back of participants' knees for three hours (knees have many blood vessels). The researchers found that they were able to alter the participants' circadian sleep/wake cycle for up to three hours. This suggests that light is a powerful exogenous zeitgeber detected by skin receptor sites and is not necessary for light to enter the eyes to influence the suprachiasmatic nucleus (SCN). The exact mechanism for this is unclear; one hypothesis is that blood chemicals could be a carrier of the light signal and take the information about day length to the master clock in the brain (SCN), which will then reset the sleep/wake rhythm.

Application questions

Q98 Read the item and then answer the question that follows.

Tom is a security officer for a large building. He has just started working the night shift, and after a week, he finds that he has difficulty sleeping during the day and is becoming tense and irritable. Tom is also worried that he is less alert during the night shift itself.

Using your knowledge of endogenous pacemakers and exogenous zeitgebers, explain Tom's experiences. **[4 marks]**

The endogenous pacemaker is our internal clock that regulates our biological rhythms, such as the sleep/wake cycle. Exogenous zeitgebers are external factors such as light/dark that can influence the endogenous pacemaker and therefore, the sleep/wake cycle.

Tom will find it difficult to sleep during the day because Tom has now started to work during the night, which is keeping him awake. This means that the endogenous pacemaker, our in-built internal circadian rhythm clock that controls our sleep/wake cycle, is no longer in synchrony with the exogenous zeitgebers of light and darkness, which help to regulate our sleep/wake cycle, and thus determine when we sleep. The conflict between endogenous pacemakers and exogenous zeitgebers can lead to negative effects, such as Tom's experiencing disrupted sleep patterns, tenseness, irritability, and lack of alertness when working at night.

Q99 Julia complains that her baby is sleeping all day and keeping her awake all night.

Using your knowledge of research into exogenous zeitgebers, discuss what Julia could do to encourage her baby to sleep more at night. **[8 marks]**

Endogenous pacemakers are internal biological 'clocks' that manage our biological rhythms. The main endogenous pacemaker is the suprachiasmatic nucleus (SCN), which is responsible for regulating our circadian rhythms, such as the sleep/wake cycle. Exogenous zeitgebers are environmental cues such as light and darkness. Zeitgebers such as light are important because they help endogenous pacemakers reset themselves against the day-and-night cycle, so that the exogenous zeitgebers and endogenous pacemaker are in synchrony, which is referred to as entrainment The SCN uses the light level to synchronise the internal biological clock each day, keeping it on a 24-hour cycle. When it is dark, the SCN sends signals to the pineal gland, triggering the gland to increase the production of the hormone melatonin, which makes us feel sleepy and thus helps induce sleep. When it is light, the SCN tells the pineal gland to produce less melatonin, thus making us feel more awake.

In order for Julia to help her baby sleep at night, she should increase the baby's production of melatonin by making sure the baby is kept in a dark room at night. For example, she can ensure the curtains are closed, and the lights are off in the bedroom. For the daytime, Julia can ensure there is light during the day, especially during the winter months when daylight is shorter, which reduces the production of melatonin. Julia could also use other exogenous zeitgebers, such as the use of social cues, for example, ensuring that verbal communication, eye contact and feeding happen more frequently in the daytime.

There is research evidence that supports the importance of light as an exogenous zeitgeber. Campbell and Murphy (1998) carried out a study to see the effect of light on the sleep/wake cycle. The researchers carried out an experiment on 15 volunteers who slept in a laboratory for four days and nights. The researchers woke the participants at various times (2 pm, 9 am, 4 am, etc.), and shone a bright light on to the back of participants' knees for three hours (knees have many blood vessels). The researchers found that they were able to alter the the participants' circadian sleep/wake cycle for up to three hours. This suggests that light is a powerful exogenous zeitgeber detected by skin receptor sites and it is not necessary for light to enter the eyes to influence the SCN. However, it could be argued that babies may not have been exposed long enough to the day-and-night cycle to be synchronised with their circadian rhythm like adults have. This suggests that the study based on adults may not be appropriate to generalise to babies.

However, the influence of exogenous zeitgebers may be overstated. Miles et al. (1977) described the case of a man blind from birth with a circadian rhythm of 24.9 hours. His sleep/wake cycle could not adjust to social cues, so he took sedatives at night and stimulants in the morning to align with the 24-hour world. Similarly, a study by Luce and Segal (1966) of individuals who live in Arctic regions (where the sun does not set during the summer months) showed that people still maintain a normal sleep pattern despite prolonged exposure to light. Both these examples suggest there are occasions when exogenous zeitgebers may have little bearing on our internal biological rhythms. Unfortunately, it would suggest that Julia's manipulation of light and dark to encourage her baby to sleep more at night may not work.

Long-response question

Q100 Outline and evaluate the effects of endogenous pacemaker and endogenous zeitgeber on the sleep/wake cycle.

[16 marks]

Endogenous pacemakers are internal biological 'clocks' that manage our biological rhythms. In humans, the main endogenous pacemaker is the suprachiasmatic nucleus (SCN), which are is a tiny cluster of nerve cells that lies in the hypothalamus and is responsible for regulating our circadian rhythms – sleep/wake cycle. The human body has other circadian clocks that are found in the cells of various organs and are referred to as peripheral circadian oscillators. The SCN is referred to as the 'master clock' as it controls, co-ordinates and synchronises all the other body circadian clocks throughout our bodies. The SCN also regulates the manufacture and secretion of the hormone melatonin in the pineal gland. The SCN sends signals to the pineal gland, triggering the gland to increase the production of melatonin when it is dark, which induces sleep. When it is lighter, the SCN triggers the pineal gland to produce less melatonin, thus making us feel more awake. Light, therefore, decreases the level of melatonin being released; the pineal and the SCN function jointly as endogenous pacemakers in the brain.

Exogenous zeitgebers are environmental cues that help to regulate circadian rhythms. The most important zeitgeber is light, as it influences our sleep/wake cycle. The SCN contains receptors that are sensitive to light. The SCN use the light level to synchronise the activity of the body's organs and glands. Light resets the internal biological clock each day, keeping it on a 24-hour cycle. Rods and cones in the retina of the eye detect light and visual images. A protein in the eye called melanopsin is sensitive to natural light. A small number of retinal cells contain melanopsin and carry signals to the SCN to set the 24-hour daily body cycle to synchronise with light and day.

The importance of endogenous pacemakers in regulating our sleep-cycle has been demonstrated in animal studies. Morgan (1995) conducted research by breeding mutant hamsters so that they had abnormal sleep/wake cycle of 20 hours rather than 24 hours. The SCN neurons from these abnormal hamsters were transplanted into the brains of normal hamsters, which as a result then displayed the same sleep/wake cycle of 20 hours. In a follow-up experiment, the SCN neurons from a normal hamster with a 24-hour sleep cycle were transplanted into the brains of the abnormal hamsters, which resulted in these hamsters having a 24-hour circadian rhythm rather than a 20-hour rhythm.

However, a limitation in the research above into endogenous pacemakers is the use of animals. For example, Morgan's research findings on hamsters may not be applicable to humans, mainly because of the physiological differences between animals and humans, but also because cognitive factors may be more significant in human biological rhythms. This means it may not be appropriate to generalise research findings on the sleep/wake cycle from animals to humans. A more disturbing issue involves the treatment of such animals (the ethics of such research), such as the cruel treatment of the hamsters in Morgan's study. Whether what is learnt from investigations on biological rhythms justifies the aversive procedures involved is a matter of debate.

There is research to show the importance of exogenous zeitgebers, such as light on our circadian rhythm. Campbell and Murphy (1998) carried out a study to see the effect light has on the sleep/wake cycle. The researchers carried out an experiment on 15 volunteers who slept in a laboratory for four days and nights. They woke the participants at various times (2 pm, 9 am, 4 am, etc.), and shone a bright light on to the back of participants' knees for three hours (knees have many blood vessels). The researchers found that they were able to alter the participants' circadian sleep/wake cycle by up to three hours. This suggests that light is a powerful exogenous zeitgeber detected by skin receptor sites and is not necessary for light to enter the eyes to influence the SCN. The exact mechanism for this is unclear; one hypothesis is that blood chemicals could be a carrier of the light signal that take the information about day length to the master clock in the brain (SCN), which will reset the sleep/wake cycle.

However, a limitation is the methodological issues in Campbell and Murphy's study. This is because their research findings have yet to be replicated by other studies - they have not produced the same results. Also, this study has been criticised because there may have been some light exposure to participants' eyes, which would be seen as a major confounding variable to the results. Furthermore, isolating one exogenous zeitgeber (light) in this way does not give insight into the many other zeitgebers that influence the sleep/wake cycle. This suggests that some studies may have underplayed the way in which different exogenous zeitgebers interact.

A final limitation is the influence of exogenous zeitgebers may be overstated. Miles et al. (1977) described the case of a man blind from birth with a circadian rhythm of 24.9 hours. His sleep/wake cycle could not adjust to social cues, so he took sedatives at night and stimulants in the morning to align with the 24-hour world. Similarly, a study by Luce and Segal (1966), of individuals who live in Arctic regions (where the sun does not set during the summer months), showed that people still maintain normal sleep patterns despite prolonged exposure to light. Both these examples suggest there are occasions when exogenous zeitgebers may have little bearing on our internal biological rhythms.

Answers to identification questions

Nervous system

Q1. A

Q2. C

Q3. B

Q4. a. (false), b. (false)

Q5. B, D

Q6. E (box 1), D (box 2)

Q7. A= sensory, B= relay neuron, C= motor neuron

Q8. (a) A, (b) C, (c) A

Endocrine system

Q20. B

Fight-or-flight response

Q24. B, C

Q25. A, B, C

Localisation of brain function

Q35. (i) A, (ii) B, (iii) D

Q36.

D = somatosensory centre

C = visual cortex

B = auditory cortex

Q.37 (a) A, (b) C, (c) D, (d) E, (e) B

Split-brain research: hemispheric lateralisation

Q51. B

Plasticity and functional recovery of the brain

Q60. C

Q61. A

Ways of studying the brain

Q68. B

Q69. B

Biological rhythms

Q81. C

Infradian and ultradian rhythms

Q86. B

Q87. B, D

Q88. A

Printed in Great Britain
by Amazon

25383295R00033